REPEAL OBAMACARE:

A Critical Look at Why It Isn't Fixable

By Jody A. Long, JD

Repeal Obamacare: A Critical Look at Why It Isn't Fixable

www.icitizenpatriot.com

ISBN-13: 978-0692227091 (BrightOwl)

ISBN-10: 0692227091

Disclaimer: *This book is written for general knowledge and is not to be substituted for legal advice. If you do have legal issues, please consult an attorney.*

Table of Contents

Despite the absence of Constitutional authority, or a single Republican vote, Obama's health care plan not only deepens the public debt, but also forces previously free citizens to purchase a product designated by the government. Never before has the federal government presumed to dictate what its citizens must buy. Moreover, Obama, and his Democrat majority in Congress, used bizarre procedures to force "ObamaCare" into law. By so doing, Obama has demonstrated that he believes his ideas on governance to be superior to the Founders', and that achieving his goals is far more important than any rules or procedural restraints. – Henry Lamb[1]

Let me start out by saying I believe health care is a right and that every citizen in the United States deserves to have affordable, quality medical care in a timely fashion. There is no reason for people with cancer or heart disease to lose their homes or to be forced into bankruptcy. We are the greatest nation on the planet and can provide for our citizens without The Affordable Patient Care Act (APC).

To clarify, the Affordable Patient Care Act is the official name of the bill H.R. 3950. It is unofficially called ObamaCare. If you see any of these designations, they refer to the same health care law. I will use generally "ObamaCare" when talking about this bill, unless it pertains to legal passage of the bill.

ObamaCare, has actually brought the health care/government issues and abuses to the forefront of the nation. Without this monstrosity, we would never have changed the abuses, unfunded liabilities, and corruption contained in the old system. Consequently, we should look at this as an opportunity to change and become a stronger, more compassionate nation. Throughout this process, we should become informed voters and only elect people who are willing to do health care the right way.

There are many myths and many government explanations of myths, which are myths in their own right. Doesn't make sense does it? It is ironic that there is so much information and disinformation out there, and most people only know what they read in Facebook or see on television. It used to be that only one in two people paid any attention to the law.[2] A recent Gallup poll shows that 33% of the people surveyed are still not familiar with the law.[3] While more people are aware that ObamaCare exists than several years ago, when the individual mandate and the other provisions start to affect them, they will want answers. In fact, they will NEED answers.

I will start by showing the legal, ethical, and practical issues contained within ObamaCare and then explain how we can design a health care system that will work.

ObamaCare – the Affordable Patient Care Act

Government control of medical care is the keystone in the arch of socialism
- Vladimir Lenin

What people heard was "free health care for everyone except the rich." What ObamaCare promised was to fight Medicare fraud while making quality insurance available to the uninsured in the U.S. These were the two main justifications given to the people for passing ObamaCare. The United States has a population of 313.9 million people according to the 2012 census. Of those people, forty-seven million citizens were uninsured. That means ObamaCare was passed to insure about 15% of the population. But if you have a closer look at who is "uninsured," many of these people can afford insurance or they choose not to sign up for government health benefits. The actual numbers of U.S. citizens who did not have access to health care is about 10 million people or 3.3% of the population. In 2019, after implementation of ObamaCare, it is estimated that 20 million people will still be without health care.[4] Meaning that ultimately, 6% more people will have health care than before ObamaCare.[5] Directly from the government website, it says that the 15% uninsured people are the ones that the ACA will affect the most.

The government response to insure 6% of the people (or affect 15% of the people) was to pass sweeping legislation that:

> "regulates activity that is commercial and economic in nature: economic and financial decisions about how and when health care is paid for, and when health insurance is purchased. In the absence of the requirement, some individuals would make an economic and financial decision to forego health insurance coverage and attempt to self-insure, which increases financial risks to households and medical providers."[6]

Between insuring 6% of the population and combating Medicare fraud, these two issues don't add up to a 1 trillion plus price tag, so what is really going on? According to Andrew McCarthy, ObamaCare is intended to serve as a temporary system to transition America to a socialized single payer system controlled by the government.[7] This is further reinforced by then Senator Obama himself in 2003. He said:

> "I happen to be a proponent of a single-payer universal health-care program. I see no reason why the United States of America, the wealthiest country in the history of the world, spending 14 percent of its gross national product on health care, cannot provide basic health insurance to everybody. Everybody in, nobody out. A single-payer health care plan, a universal health care plan. That's what I'd like to see. But as all of you know, we may not get there immediately."

ObamaCare was sold to the public as a way to have the uninsured covered under a nationally controlled health insurance. Another selling point was that the Affordable Patient Care Act would pay for itself. We were also told it wasn't a tax, but yet it would raise $143 billion dollars of revenue from taxes to be used to pay down the deficit.

According to Andrew C. McCarthy, over time, ObamaCare is designed to (a) push all Americans into government markets that are a conglomerate of Medicare, Medicaid, and "exchanges" run by state and federal agencies; (b) dictates the content of the "private" insurance product; (c) sets the price; (d) micromanages patient access, business practices, and fees of doctors; and (e) rations medical care. Concurrently, ObamaCare is designed to create a financial crisis into the system such that socialized medicine will become the only solution available.[8]

There are several ways to look at H.R. 3950 (the Affordable Patient Care Act) starting with the way it was passed by Congress and then upheld by the Supreme Court. Then I will talk about the provisions in the bill itself. It is easy to criticize a law, but that doesn't solve the problem. There are some creative solutions that will allow each State to use their 10th Amendment right to reject ObamaCare and profit as a premier health care state.

UnConstitutionality of ObamaCare

> *Article. I.* ***Section. 7.*** *- All Bills for raising Revenue shall originate in the House of Representatives; but the Senate may propose or concur with Amendments as on other Bills.*
>
> *Article. I.* ***Section. 8.*** *The Congress shall have Power To lay and collect Taxes, Duties, Imposts and Excises, to pay the Debts and provide for the common Defence and general Welfare of the United States; but all Duties, Imposts and Excises shall be uniform throughout the United States;*
>
> *Article. I.* ***Section. 8.*** *To make all Laws which shall be necessary and proper for carrying into Execution the foregoing Powers, and all other Powers vested by this Constitution in the Government of the United States, or in any Department or Officer thereof.*
>
> *Article. I.* ***Section. 8.*** *To regulate Commerce with foreign Nations, and among the several States, and with the Indian Tribes.*

There are several reasons why the ruling on ObamaCare is irregular and therefore the law is unconstitutional.

ObamaCare was tried on **one** issue of unconstitutionality, which was the individual mandate. The case is *National Federation of Independent Business v. Sebelius*, 567 U.S. ___ (2012). The individual mandate means that all citizens must participate in ObamaCare or they would be fined. That doesn't mean that **all** the constitutional issues are settled. The individual mandate issue before the Court looks at whether the government has the power to penalize all U.S. citizens for inactivity.

The separation of powers doctrine means that the Judiciary cannot perform duties assigned to the legislature. Although the doctrine of judicial review is not an enumerated power in the Constitution, the Supreme Court claimed this power in the early 1800's and now has a long history of reviewing laws for constitutionality. These two doctrines show that only the legislature can write laws and that the Court can only say whether a law is Constitutional or not. Chief Justice Roberts does not have the authority under the Constitution or doctrine of judicial review to reform or re-write a law. If a law is deemed unconstitutional, then it must go back to Congress for constitutional corrections if lawmakers want the law to be enforceable.

The government argued that the individual mandate penalty was not a tax so that it would be procedurally valid according to the Constitution. The argument put forth by the government was that since all Americans inevitably consume health care as a matter of commerce, that Congress can compel people to pay for their care with government approved insurance. The Senate justified passage of ObamaCare via congressional power to "regulate commerce among the states." Senate justification was further amplified by the power to pass all laws that are "necessary and proper" to execute implementation of ObamaCare.

The Supreme Court responded by telling Congress that it is an improper use of legislative power to justify the individual mandate through the commerce clause or the necessary and proper clause. Remarkably, the court put boundaries around the practically limitless power of these two Constitutional clauses that Congress has carved out for itself. The other nugget of power the Supreme Court gave the States is when it cautioned that Congress could not use the spending power clause to justify coercing states to either accept the Medicaid expansion or risk losing existing Medicaid funding.

The Supreme Court heard arguments on four issues: 1) the Individual Mandate, 2) the Tax Anti-injunction Act, 3) Severability, and 4) Medicaid. Ironically, the tax issue was not argued before the Supreme Court, yet it was the issue that it was decided on. Chief Justice Roberts legislated from the bench. He reformed the law by declaring that the individual mandate was a tax. So while the individual mandate was upheld as constitutional, the door of unconstitutionality was opened because as a tax, it did not originate in the House pursuant to Article I Section 7.

The Supreme Court stated that the purpose of the individual mandate is to force healthy people to buy expensive health plans to subsidize insurance companies.[9] By forcing the 'young invincibles' to participate via the individual mandate, these people would fund the health insurances to provide coverage to people with chronic illnesses and pre-existing conditions. In other words, the healthy people have a government-mandated tax to subsidize everyone else while turning the insurers into private tax collectors.

One of the long accepted principles for interpreting the U.S. Constitution is that powers are narrow, rights are broad.[10] This means that the power of the U.S. government to enforce an individual mandate should be narrowly interpreted. Yet the right of individuals to control their health care decisions, which is part of their personal rights via the 10th Amendment, should be broadly construed. The presumption is in favor of the rights of the people and the burden of proof is on the Government since they are claiming the power. The Supreme Court spent more time focusing on the Government having the right to tax people rather than the real issue of whether the Government had the power to put a penalty tax on the people. The U.S. Constitution only allows for duties (tax on import or export of goods), imposts (tax on imports), and excise taxes via Article I, Section 8, Clause 1, and the income tax via the 16 Amendment. Narrowly construed, a penalty tax does not fall under any of these enumerated powers, and so the individual mandate should be struck down.

One of my personal issues with the individual mandate is where will the government stop once this precedent is enforced? Today its health care, tomorrow we can be individually mandated to buy government trucks for bailouts, bank at government approved banks, or use educational monopolies backed by the government. The other issue is pure economics. Why would a young, healthy person want to subsidize health insurances by handing them $400/mth + a $5,000 deductible ($9800) when they might spend $500 per year to have tests and see a doctor?

I also think a constitutional argument can be made that individual mandates need to be geographically uniform and applied with the "same force and effect in every place where the subject is found."[11] While it is true that the penalty itself may be consistent, it is not true that the premium for the uninsured is consistent throughout the State exchanges. Because premiums differ according to each state, the cost to avoid the individual mandate is not uniformly applied.

Another matter of judicial procedure is that a judge must recuse himself or herself from a case in the event they would be predisposed to rule in favor of one of the parties prior to hearing all the evidence. This doctrine has to do with fundamental fairness against bias in the case. Another reason judges recuse themselves is if there is a conflict of interest. Justice Kagan should have recused herself because she had a clear bias in favor of ObamaCare.[12] She had previously written a published paper in favor of nationalized medicine. Additionally, since she was Obama's personal attorney prior to being appointed to the bench and Obama had so much invested in nationalizing medicine, there is a clear conflict of interest.

The Supreme Court has issues on many levels. The actual opinion itself rewrites the law and is outside the scope of power delegated by the Constitution because only the Congress can write a law. When the Supreme Court called the mandate a tax, this invalidates the ACA because any matters of taxation must be raised in the House of Representatives in order for it to be constitutional. (Discussed in the Legislative Branch issues below) The procedural issues of judicial bias and conflict of interest makes the ObamaCare ruling void because procedurally, the hearing must be fair and unbiased. In this case, it was not a fair or unbiased decision.

Individual Mandate

ObamaCare is based on forcing people into the federal monopoly via an insurance third-party payer model. In order for the system to work, it must have people who are not sick to pay for those who are chronically sick. This is an income transfer. If the system does not have enough money to pay for the chronically sick people, then insurances loses a lot of money. The individual mandate was the lynch pin holding the legislation together. That is why it was so important for the Supreme Court to uphold ObamaCare - to keep the individual mandate in place so that the entire legislation didn't fail for lack of money and control over everyone.

Interestingly, the government website says that it doesn't create a government-run health care system or government insurance.[13] This statement is misleading. Since the health insurance industry must follow extensive and many times overreaching government mandates, the health insurances are government actors with very little leeway to act on their own merits. The amount of control the government has over health insurance, premiums, coverage, reports, information, doctors, nurses, medical staff, prescriptions, community health centers, student loans, and many other intertwining health care-related issues, effectively turns private entities into government actors. DHHS even has Exchanges signing people up to vote with "Democrat" boxes already selected for them.[14]

It is also misleading to believe the statement that "ObamaCare regulates insurance not health care"[15] or that "health care is in the hands of you and your doctor." Generally, doctors and hospitals will do what they are paid to do. Insurances, Medicare and Medicaid determine what doctors, pharmacies, and hospitals will be paid. DHHS agency regulations and other government mechanisms control these payments. While your doctor can recommend a treatment, if it is too expensive or not on a prescription formulary, chances are good that insurance, Medicare, or Medicaid will not pay for it. That means that indirectly these government actors are substituting their opinion for what is necessary for cutting medical costs as opposed to the doctor's independent judgment as to what is best for the patient. It is not just between you and your doctor, unless you have the financial means to afford it yourself.

The government also controls all the consumers through the individual mandate penalty tax, affecting all citizens. When you control all the consumers and most of the actors of the health care system it is hard to say that this is not government run, which by definition is a socialist health care system.

Here, the Supreme Court failed to protect the people and failed to enforce the important separation of powers doctrine. This erodes the confidence of the people in a system that should provide a check on the undue pressure from an executive branch and malfeasant legislative branch. I have more faith in the will of the people to vote for repeal of ObamaCare than I do in a politically charged judicial branch to protect the people and uphold the Constitution.

ObamaCare Issues – Executive Branch

The separation of powers doctrine contained in the Constitution is meant to ensure that the judicial, legislative, and the executive branches of government have equal power. Each branch of government was provided with checks and balances so that no branch would become more powerful than the other two branches. The Founding Fathers highlighted the separation of powers doctrine as a mechanism to maintain a democratic government. The only branch that can make laws is Congress. The President cannot make laws and is not to put undue pressure on the other branches to pass laws to further his agenda.

I will discuss executive pressure on the Senate Democrats in the next section.

In a nutshell, Ted Cruz, a Congressman of Texas, has listed Executive Branch abuses regarding Obamacare[16]:

1. Granted a "hardship" exemption from the individual mandate for people whose health plans were canceled because their plans weren't Obamacare compliant.[17]
2. Delayed the individual mandate for two years.[18]
3. Allowed individuals to buy health insurance plans in 2014 that did not comply with Obamacare.[19] Extended this delay until 2016 - past the mid-term elections.[20]
4. Extended the deadline to enroll in the ACA.[21]
5. Illegally granted businesses a waiver from Obamacare's employer mandate.[22] Twice.[23]
6. Illegally continued the Obamacare employer contribution for congressional staffs.[24]
7. Illegally delayed the Obamacare caps on out-of-pocket health care payments.[25]
8. Illegally delayed Obamacare verification of eligibility for health care subsidies.[26]
9. Illegally required people to violate their faith via the Obamacare contraception mandate.[27]
10. As of May 2011, over 50% of Obamacare waiver beneficiaries were union members (who account for less than 12% of the American work force).[28]

Executive branch pressure on the Supreme Court has to do with oddness and reports of threatening to suspend money for Medicare. Originally, Chief Justice Roberts had written the majority of the conservative position that turned out to be the dissent. When he swung to the other side, he also wrote, in large part, the majority opinion. This was such an odd change at the last minute that many speculate he was inordinately pressured from outside of the court. Whether there was a threat, personal or otherwise, we'll never know. However, it was reported that Obama warned the Supreme Court that they had better rule in his favor or elderly people would suffer as a consequence of federal withholding of Medicare payments to doctors and hospitals.[29] While many people would say that the government arguments were brilliantly persuasive, I can tell you from many years of courtroom experiences that Judges rarely have a radical change from their initial positions. I'm not saying it isn't possible. I'm just saying it is rare enough to be suspect.

The Constitution does not mention executive orders. Executive Orders are those orders issued by the President to faithfully execute the laws passed by Congress.[30] Executive orders cannot rewrite the law or be arbitrary or capricious in choosing which laws of Congress to follow. When the executive branch claims too much power, the other branches of government must challenge it. Failure to challenge improper usage of executive orders carries too high a risk that a dictator President will replace the Constitution.

The President does not have the authority to change the law, not even a little bit. Congress included specific deadlines in the Affordable Patient Care Act (ACA). If the particular deadlines cannot be met, then it is up to Congress to change the effective dates. As of February 2014, there were a total of 28 deadlines missed.[31]

There was so much uproar about people losing their health insurance that Obama unilaterally demanded insurances to "un-cancel" the health insurance plans. The ACA stated that effective January 1, 2014, health insurance policies that did not meet new government regulations or that were not grandfathered in by law would be cancelled. That meant that if a person had a health insurance policy they were happy with but it didn't cover gender changes or contraception, that they would lose their health insurance effective January 1, 2014. People who were covered by the 6.2 million cancelled health insurance policies represent a lot of voters. Obama used the executive order to change the date that substandard policies would become unlawful. The new date is January 1, 2015, after the November elections.[32] Congress was prepared to change the date to January 1, 2015, but because Republicans had brought up the fix, Obama threatened to veto it.[33]

President Obama unilaterally delayed the individual mandate until after the 2016 presidential elections by offering Americans a "hardship exemption."[34] People owning any of the 6.2 million cancelled policies and who couldn't afford the new insurance premiums under ObamaCare qualify for the hardship exemption. Interestingly, this new category that defines a hardship can also apply if "you consider other available policies unaffordable." Theoretically, people can get a hardship exemption for unspecified reasons, which requires "documentation if possible."[35] This will ensure that people are not penalized immediately for failure to comply with the mandate until after elections.

Another executive order pertained to the employer mandate. The order delayed implementation for small businesses. Employers with fewer than 100 workers do not have to provide health insurance until 2016. The IRS, part of the executive branch, said larger firms have to cover at least 70% of the workforce starting in 2015. Another business-related provision is that employers cannot provide better health insurance for top executives than what is offered to regular employees or they will owe a fine of $100/day. Obama unilaterally delayed IRS enforcement of this provision too.[36]

Another one of the President's power grabs is by appointing Czars as an end run around Congress. Czars are people who are put in positions of extreme power who are not elected. Many are not even confirmed by Congress. Most of the Czars have no accountability to the people or anyone else except for the president. They typically have a lot of power to further the presidential agenda. In the case of the Secretary, she is appointed as the Health Care Czar. However, because she is appointed as head of the Department of Health Services, she does have some accountability via the court system, the president, and Congress. Appendix A shows the extent of her duties and power to implement the ACA.

Obama has also been putting pressure on U.S. citizens. By virtue of being at the top of the executive branch, President Obama has sanctioned agency persecution of those people who disagree with his policies, like Christians, seniors, Medicare recipients, legal gun owners, Veterans, and the Tea Party. He also does not have a problem with changing the law or selectively enforcing it to help his supporters. For instance, Obama recently assured Hispanics that if they lived in a mixed family of legal and illegal status that signing up for ObamaCare would not result in their loved ones being deported.[37] Obama defended outrageous premiums for 'affordable' health care by telling already economically strapped Americans that they needed to reorganize their budgets by canceling their cable or cell phones to pay into the ObamaCare leviathan. It is far too overreaching for the government to tell the people what sanctioned government product they must buy or how to spend their household money.

Given the undue executive branch influence on the judicial branch, the legislative branch, and the people, ObamaCare fails the separation of powers doctrine contained in the U.S. Constitution. The unilateral changes rewriting congressional laws are also a violation of the Constitution, especially when these changes are deliberately made to change the course of elections. While pressure on the American people is not against the Constitution, it is against the law to stifle political free speech and to misuse political power to punish those that oppose the President's agenda. It is also unconstitutional to selectively enforce congressional laws. The elephant in the room is that the unilateral policy regarding enforcement of the mandates is a delicate matter towards Democrats keeping their power. The mandates will be enforced, but only after elections when the American people can't do anything about it.

ObamaCare Issues – Legislative Branch

The Constitution was written in a way to ensure separation of powers so that no one branch of the government is more powerful than the others. It is a check and balance system that is meant to be a protection for the people. The legislative process is specifically set up in a way to protect the minority of the people from the tyranny of the majority. Built into the system is a means for debate in both the House and the Senate. This allows for the best wording and expression of legislation so that is for the good of the people they represent. Accordingly, debate in two houses of Congress is supposed to be another layer of protection for the people governed by these laws, especially when these laws tremendously affect the entire nation.

There was a lot of improper legislative maneuvering through the democratically controlled Senate.

The first bill was drafted in the House and entitled The Affordable Health Care for America Act (HR 3962). Although it passed the House, it did not pass the Senate so it was dropped.

The House passed a 6-page bill called the Service Members Home Ownership Tax Act of 2009 (HR 3590).[38] There is no mention of an individual mandate or of national health care. When HR3590 went to the Senate, it was "Amended." The first paragraph says that the initial act for Service Members is tabled, and removes all six pages voted and approved of from the House of Representatives. Then under the auspices of Harry Reid, the Senate inserted 2076 pages and changed the name of the bill to Patient Protection and Affordable Care Act.[39] Although technically the same bill number (HR3950) that originated in the House, there was nothing of the original bill remaining in the amendment. The bill passed the Senate on December 24, 2009, through a procedurally improper mechanism called reconciliation.

The Senate tried to justify their power to raise revenue (aka the individual mandate language) by attaching to the individual through the "necessary and proper" clause and the "commerce" clause. This rationale supposedly gave HR3590 the constitutional authority to originate in the Senate and to bypass the constitutional checks and balances. The Supreme Court later ruled that neither, the necessary and proper clause nor the interstate commerce clause, gives Congress the power to attach the individual mandate to the individual.

The Senate Democrats knew they wouldn't get HR3590 through the House using the normally required legislative procedure. Nancy Pelosi came up with the idea that the Senate should pass the law through the reconciliation process and deem it passed in the House. On one hand, they promised the House that they could pass an amendment to ObamaCare, while the Senate simultaneously passed HR1203.[40] HR1203 effectively muzzled the House by severely limiting debate time and who could submit an amendment to HR3950.[41]

Reconciliation is a process for Congress to expedite budget-related legislation. This method allows for a simple majority approval of 51% and cannot be filibustered.[42] This procedure is not intended for a bill that affects so much of the gross national product or medical, pharmaceutical, and insurance industries.

The House ratified the Senate Amendment (HR3950) through The Health Care and Education Reconciliation Act (HR 4872). The House amendment (HR4872) was part of the reconciliation procedure to amend ObamaCare (HR3950) with 55 pages of minor changes to dates and amounts.

Inserted into this bill was language to the effect that ObamaCare could only be repealed during a specified time or it would remain as law of the land.[43] Congress tried to give the ACA more authority than an Amendment to the Constitution, which still can be repealed by popular vote.

The House did not vote on the contents of HR3950, nor did they have a chance to debate the provisions contained in the 906-page monstrosity. The House only voted on the amendments to the amendment. On March 21, 2010, the House voted on HR4872. The bill was barely passed with 220 in favor to 211 against.[44] Not one single Republican in the House ratified ObamaCare or voted for this Reconciliation Amendment.[45] The ACA was signed by Obama on March 23, 2010.[46] The ACA was unilaterally passed by the Democrats in both the Senate and the House.

To ease the voter backlash concerning the House Democrats, Pelosi came up with the idea of "deeming" the bill passed.[47] That way when angry voters confronted their Congressperson for casting a vote in favor of ObamaCare, they could have plausible deniability. The Democrats in the House of Representatives could truthfully say that they didn't vote for ObamaCare because they only voted on the amendment of ObamaCare.

But according to the Obama health law, any bill to abolish it must be introduced in Congress in one miniscule time window, January 1 to February 1, 2017 and must be enacted by August 15 of that year. This provision is highly unconstitutional since no Congress can bind a future Congress. The proper procedure for a semi-permanent law is to make it in the form of a Constitutional amendment. But even that can still be overturned with a 2/3 majority of votes.

Now fast-forward to the Supreme Court decision on June 28, 2012, that upheld the individual mandate as a tax. As such, the U.S. Constitution states:

> **Article I, Section 7:** All Bills for raising Revenue shall originate in the House of Representatives.

The Supreme Court decision on the individual mandate made ObamaCare unconstitutional because a tax is a bill that raises revenue and it did not originate in the House of Representatives. HR3590 was a number that started in the House, but the legislation itself did not originate in the House. Furthermore, the House bill did not have any provisions that remotely resembled the language that the

Senate inserted into the bill. So did the Senate amend the bill? Yes, but only to make the bill a clean slate. Then they substituted their own bill into the original bill. This is bad faith, purposely done to get something through the legislative process that would never have gotten through both branches of Congress had they transparently followed the Constitution.

Congress only has the power to levy taxes that fall under certain categories like excise, impost, apportioned, or income tax through the 16th Amendment. Nowhere does Congress have the power to order a legislative penalty, akin to a constitutionally prohibited Bill of Attainder. But then again, they greased their way around this saying that non-compliance doesn't rise to the level of a crime. It is only a monetary penalty, like an infraction fine.

Right now, a monetary penalty that is only enforced by the IRS withholding tax refunds might not sound bad. But when have you ever seen the government stop at collection efforts by only seizing an IRS refund? Consider if a person gets enough speeding or parking tickets, it will rise to the level of a habitual offender and result in criminal penalties. Social security was once a 'voluntary' program. Now it is mandatory. Income tax was supposed to be temporary to pay for war debt. Now it is mandatory. The government made laws protecting banks, so Student Loans are now the most oppressive loans in history. Even the NSDA that was passed with the intention of government reaching terrorists in the U.S. has been used as an excuse to spy on every U.S. citizen. The government has a long history of expanding taxes and power over citizens.

The ACA affected so much of our GDP and fundamentally changed America. It was passed through an improper budgetary procedure that lowered the number of votes needed to pass the legislation. Not one Republican voted for the ACA or the Reconciliation Act, so it wasn't bipartisan. HR3950 was never debated in Congress. The Democrats had control of the House, the Senate, and the Presidency, subjecting the minority to the tyranny of the bare majority with only seven votes. No Congressperson read and understood all that was contained in the 906 pages of HR3950. There were many last minute changes and additions to the law. Pelosi told the Senate they'd have to vote for it to know what was in it. This is a classic case of taxation without representation. For all these irregularities, ObamaCare is illegal and should be declared 100% unconstitutional or repealed, whichever can happen soonest.

The 4th Branch of Government - Agencies

Under the separation of powers provisions in the Constitution, delegation of congressional power is implied. Congressional delegation power is not expressly granted. The Supreme Court, under Chief Justice John Marshall, held that Congress could delegate power so long as the rulemaking concerned the "mere details" of implementing the legislation on important issues passed by Congress.[48] Further clarification constrained Congress to "common sense delegation" and the "inherent necessities" of the situation.[49] In *Mistretta v. United States* (1989), the Supreme Court enlarged agency power by holding that delegation of power was constitutional if Congress specifies the "general policy, the agency the power is delegated to, and the boundaries of the delegated power." While this is an oversimplification of the delegation power issue, it provides a basis for understanding agencies. The Court has increasingly granted broader delegation power since *Mistretta*, and provided boundaries in the case of standardless delegations of power in only the worst of circumstances.

The agency trend of ever-increasing delegation of power enables abuse of power that is not easily controlled and that is fairly unaccountable to the people. Agencies are like little fiefdoms with a lot of rulemaking discretion and power to implement congressional policies. The people do not elect agency heads. Rulemaking is complicated and rarely watched by the public. For instance, March 1, DHHS released 700 pages to explain four rules regarding

ObamaCare.[50] How many people are going to take the time to read and comment on all 700 pages? Only in rare instances where the person or entity is charged with violating agency rules and has a lot of money, is there a chance to overturn these rules. Realistically, most of the time these rules stand, and over time the precedent stacks up in favor of agency rules being accurate as assessed by the agency.

How does delegation of power apply to ObamaCare? The short answer is that it is a transfer of power over medicine, health care, insurance, citizens and the government. It also significantly changes the relationship (i.e. power and money) between States, citizens, and the Federal Government. Depending on what figures you use, this amounts to a transfer of power and money of one-fifth to one-third of the gross domestic product of the United States.

Three primary agencies have tremendous power. They are the Department Health and Human Service (DHHS), the Internal Revenue Service (IRS), and the Department of Justice (DOJ). The DHHS has the bulk of the rulemaking power to implement ObamaCare. Both the IRS and DOJ, are part of the executive arm of enforcing the law.

Department of Health and Human Services (DHHS)

In ObamaCare, the Secretary of Department of Health and Human Services (DHHS) has a lot of power. Out of the 906 pages delegating power to the DHHS, the Secretary so far has promulgated over 20,000 pages of agency law to implement ObamaCare. According to the Citizens' Council on Health Care, ObamaCare delegates power to the Secretary:

"Secretary"	3267 times
"Secretary shall"	1051 times
"By the Secretary"	651 times
"Secretary may"	371 times
"Secretary determines"	222 times
"Secretary under"	80 times
"Secretary in consultation"	39 times [51]

The power contained in the office of one unelected official is staggering. Here is a partial list of the delegated power: medical reimbursement to doctors, determine the criteria for qualified health plans, waivers, Medicaid, CHIP, enrollment, IPAB Boards, hospital reimbursement, drug formularies, restaurant food labeling, nursing homes, Medicare, massive data integration with at least 159 boards and agencies, prescriptions, and the individual mandate. Of these numerous agencies, organizations, and programs created from ObamaCare they will need to promulgate their own rules.[52] Several of these entities are granted powers to create other organizations, making this an administrative nightmare over the citizens it is supposed to serve.

The full list of powers delegated to the Secretary is contained in Appendix A. Some of those powers are fairly broad such as the Secretary can impose any regulation to "improve health care quality."[53] The full list of boards and agencies created in the ACA is contained in Appendix B. Among these boards, she has full power to create evidentiary privileges and confidentiality of communication.[54]

The Secretary can directly influence insurances and premiums. She has the power to decide what is included in a "qualified health plan" or what constitutes "minimum essential benefits." Any insurance that does not meet these standards is not part of the health care exchange system. Since the Secretary is in charge of insurance exchanges, her rating system and evaluation of the plans allows her to effectively steer consumers towards certain insurances and plans.

The powers not delegated to the United States by the Constitution, nor prohibited by it to the States, are reserved to the States respectively, or to the people.

In the U.S. Bill of Rights, there is a protection against an exercise of improper federal power over the states via the 10th Amendment.

I will go into more detail about States' rights below, but for now, I bring this up because ObamaCare designates agency power over the States. It is also troubling that if the Secretary determines that a State will not have a functioning exchange by January 1, 2014, "the Secretary shall (directly or through agreement with a not-for-profit entity) establish and operate such Exchange within the State and the Secretary shall take such actions as are necessary to implement such other requirements."[55] Consequently, the Secretary has power to not only interfere in a State's existing plan, but to insert the agency will over the state's sovereignty.

Moreover, there is a lot of money flowing through DHHS and it is the Secretary's prerogative on who is selected for the billions of dollars of grant money.

Just about every section of the ACA calls for one or more reports. What they will do with that tremendous amount of data, if they get it at all, will be highly suspect since there is a total lack of accountability built into the system. If the past is an indicator of the future, they will take the money, create a lot of bureaucracy, but in the end, nothing will be done and nobody will be accountable for any failures to achieve goals of the reports.[56] People should be demanding refunds of all money that is unaccounted for from companies who fail to submit reports or take the money and go bankrupt afterwards.

The Internal Revenue Service is part of the executive branch because it regulates and penalizes for failure to comply with the individual mandates. The IRS also promulgates numerous rules. They also have their numerous rules they have promulgated. A current hot button concerns state exchanges.[57] As it stands, the States can participate by setting up their own health care exchanges. Since the federal government cannot force or coerce the states to participate, any state that chooses not to opt in, their citizens can choose to participate in the federal exchange. So far, about 34 States have chosen not to opt in, but that number changes over time.

Another related Supreme Court challenge also has to do with consumers signing up for ObamaCare. Health care tax credits (aka premium subsidies) are tied to language in the statute that says that health care subsidies can only be claimed if the consumer goes through the state exchanges. It is estimated that 85% of enrollees need the subsidies to afford to buy ObamaCare insurance.[58] This language becomes problematic for those who signed up in the federal exchange because most of these people would not be able to afford ObamaCare without the subsidies. This means that according to the ACA, only consumers in the 16 participating states can get subsidies. Pursuant to the statute, the remaining people who signed up through the federal exchange were not supposed to receive premium subsidies.

The legislative history shows that Congress wanted to give the States an incentive to participate in individual state exchanges rather than relying on the federal exchange or opting out altogether. The language in HR 3950 reflects that incentive by giving subsidies to the people who sign up through the state exchanges. This issue is important because both, the individual mandate and the employer business mandate, are tied to the health care tax credits. Employers in States that do not participate in the exchanges would not be penalized for failing to offer qualified insurance plans. This gives them a significant financial advantage over employers in participating States.

Subsidies make ObamaCare workable so people can afford health insurance. If the enrollees do not get subsidies and cannot afford health insurance, then they fall under the hardship exemption, meaning they will not have to buy insurance or pay the individual mandate. If people cannot afford to sign up for ObamaCare, then ultimately, they will skew the insurance pool so that it has many more chronically sick participants than healthy, paying participants. If that happens, the legislation fails. Consequently, there are two very important reasons why Congress was giving subsidies to people participating in state exchanges. The legislation was written to encourage the individual mandate and the employer mandate to attach to more people and states in order to keep the legislation from financially failing.

The U.S. Constitution gives implied powers to the executive branch. These implied powers are "only to 'carry into Execution' an expressed power and not to do whatever is necessary to achieve the intent for which a power might be exercised."[59] In other words, the ends doesn't justify the means – the delegatee still needs to stay within the grant of limited power.

For instance, the IRS thinks they have the power to rewrite laws to keep ObamaCare from failing. Only Congress can write laws. The IRS promulgated a rule saying that the premium subsidies also apply to people who enroll through the federal exchange. The IRS justified this interpretation because they say that Congress made a clerical or drafting error. The IRS is outside of their scope of delegation power to rewrite the rule by ignoring the plain language of the law and the legislative intent. In other words, "the IRS is attempting to create two entitlements not authorized by Congress and, in the process, to tax employers and individuals whom Congress did not authorize the agency to tax."[60]

The economic substance doctrine contained in ObamaCare is expected to net $4.5 billion dollars by giving the IRS unfettered discretion to call taxpayers liars. The IRS can disallow legal tax deductions by "deeming that the 'action lacks substance' and is merely intended to reduce taxes owed."[61] The door is wide open for arbitrary and capricious application of the economic substance doctrine.

Department of Justice

Another agency that has threatened to weigh in on ObamaCare is the Department of Justice (DOJ). Many people are losing their health insurance, their jobs, or their working hours are reduced as a direct consequence of ObamaCare employer mandate on tax consequences on a set number of full-time employees. Businesses run on a bottom line. To give you an idea of the jump in personnel costs, ObamaCare added $7,000,000 to the cost of doing business for AOL.[62] To stay in business, corporations will take the cheapest alternative. To avoid ObamaCare, for some businesses it is cheaper to pay the $2,000 penalty per employee than to pay the exorbitant cost of a "qualified health plan" that covers the "minimum essential benefits." Thus, they cancel insurance that they may have otherwise had available for their employees. For other businesses, it is cheaper to have less employees or to have part-time employees who do not meet the federal definition of full-time (30 hours). Consequently, these people will lose their jobs or have their income severely diminished by reduced hours available to work.

Obama told businesses they couldn't make business decisions to get out of paying for ObamaCare. The DOJ is backing him up by criminally prosecuting businesses if they provide a false certification that their staffing decisions were not motivated by ObamaCare.[63]

As scary as the preceding discussion on agencies might be, my biggest point is that no matter what ObamaCare says, the 906 pages doesn't really matter much. Much of the way ObamaCare is written has a lot of feel-good language and provides a lot of carrots to get States and people to buy into the program. A select few states and organizations have readily taken the carrots such that many of the funds are now depleted. For example, gone are the $5 billion dollars allocated to help states cover enrollees with pre-existing conditions or the $5 billion dollars in reinsurance for early retirees.[64] This money helped entice states to sign up for the ACA. It also helped many corporations, unions, and states to fund their public retirement (discontinued in 2011). The problems are that most of money for deal sweeteners has already been awarded to a select few and mechanisms like waivers or delays are only temporary until after elections.

The bottom line is that the government was willing to promise just about anything to Democrats and their supporters to get a national health care program in place. These deals are reflected in the text of ObamaCare and several bills that were passed around the time of the Affordable Patient Care Act. The devil is in the details and the details are what make ObamaCare truly scary. Already there are over 20,000 pages of regulations with just DHHS alone and they aren't done yet.[65] We have to contend with unjust and unconstitutional ways of how the IRS and the DOJ want to enforce ObamaCare. What other rules and regulations are the 159 other agencies and boards going to pass? Do we, as U.S. citizens, really want to be subjected to all that regulation and forced to pay for whatever the government wants us to buy?

States' Rights

Have you ever wondered why the dollar has an eagle with 13 arrows in the talon? It means that the individual 13 colonies are separate but equal. It also means that they can defend themselves better when banded together, similar to the ideas of the sovereign Iroquois tribes who were separate but banded together. Another example is the European Union (EU). None of the countries that belong to this economically feasible union renounced their sovereignty to the EU. They still have their separate identities.

Generally, powers not delegated to the Federal government in the Constitution are reserved to the States respectively, or to the people via the 10th Amendment. Consider that whenever groups of people come together, each one of those groups have 100% of the power to negotiate on behalf of the people. If the representatives of the group create an agreement to accomplish a goal, each person in the group is bound to the agreement due to delegating authority to the representative of the group. Absent a delegation of power to the group that agrees to relieve group members of all rights, the group representatives cannot promise more than what authority they have been given. In property law, they call this a remainder. In contract law, they call this delegation of power or authority in agency/partnership law. The individuals and the group of individuals will retain their individuality and their sovereignty in any grant of power unless they agree to a total divesting of their power.

Similarly, it is that way for the Colonies when they joined as the United States under one Constitution. Great Britain had historically gotten increasingly more tyrannical over the colonies and the states were throwing off the yoke of oppression. The colonies wanted to be independent of any rulers. To further emphasize that fact, States wanted to ensure that individuals and the States were protected from Federal overreaching by drafting a Bill of Rights. Constitutional history shows that the Founding Fathers and other leaders of the States felt that if they had divested their power to the government, they would have seen it like trading one monarchy for another. The Constitution and the Bill of Rights derive their power from the people via the States.

That is a key principal behind Nullification.[66] In the event the Constitutional checks and balances do not protect the people, the States retained the power to be the ultimate decider of unconstitutional laws. Through Nullification, States are exercising their sovereignty that they entered into the Constitution with. States are the ultimate decider regarding constitutionality.

I really wish I could say that the checks and balances system of the Supreme Court, Congress, and the President was a fair and just balance of power. Unfortunately, the reality is that the Supreme Court is stacked, most of Congress is either stacked or the servant of special interest groups or big money, and we have a President who has an anti-American agenda.

Few if any law schools will mention Nullification in constitutional law classes and there is a lot of controversy surrounding the concept. Moreover, there is a disturbing trend among progressives to pick which parts of the Constitution they want to enforce and ignore other parts by saying times have changed.

Slavery is held out as an example. While it is true that slavery was a reality when the Constitution was drafted, it does not mean the Constitution is flawed. The Founders did what they needed to do to get all States to agree to sign the document. The Founders drafted a procedure in the Constitution that would allow for changes in the event the majority of the people wanted changes. The desire for alcohol and voting rights legally changed the Bill of Rights. Likewise, if health care was a pressing issue for the majority of the people, they could legally vote to amend the Constitution. The amendment process is a protection against a runaway government like the one we have today.

People think nullification was only a Civil War idea, but there are numerous examples throughout U.S. history. The most notable example from the past was the Sedition Act said that the government could not be criticized. States ignored this law and it was repealed due to popular refusal to follow the law. Prohibition was another example. Currently, we see many States passing laws against the enforcement of ObamaCare and gun control. These are a form of nullification; it does not have to be as extreme as succession.

DHHS has sent letters to Oklahoma, Missouri, Texas, and Wyoming that they will enforce ObamaCare in the respective States.[67] As noted above, the ACA gives DHHS the power to set up federal exchange in those States and to enforce implementation. But, the Supreme Court said that States do not have to participate and cannot be coerced by the Federal government. Missouri's response is that they are in the process of passing a law that not only declares the ACA unconstitutional, but also creates criminal penalties for persons enforcing or attempting to enforce the act in the state of Missouri. Similarly, Georgia[68] and Ohio[69] passed protections against enforcing ObamaCare in their states.

The insurance agency has historically been a matter left to the States. Oklahoma is confronting the federal government through the insurance commission by claiming costly and excessive burdens from dual regulation. Oklahoma's position is that the insurance commission does not have the authority to enforce federal laws that are inconsistent with the Oklahoma Constitution and statutes. The DHHS response was that they wanted "establishment of a 'collaborative enforcement arrangement.' This deal would permit the feds to force ObamaCare on Oklahomans while allowing the Oklahoma Insurance Department (OID) to ostensibly keep its hands clean."[70]

As most people know, ObamaCare was fashioned on the Massachusetts model, also known as RomneyCare. The main distinction between ObamaCare and RomneyCare is that one is a national health care plan and the other is a state health care solution. As much as it pains me, I do support a State's decision to impose health care on its citizens because it is legally a State's right to do so. Vermont has decided to comply with most of ObamaCare. Instead of going through insurances for payment, they will set up a government-managed system to collect all the health care fees and to pay out all the health care costs. In order to do this, Green Mountain Care will not be able completely launch until 2017 because the health care exchange still needs approval from the federal government to use federal money to fund the state program.[71]

Maryland just wasted $125 Million dollars trying to interface through the federal ObamaCare exchange. Now, they will use technology from Connecticut's marketplace.[72] Hawaii's ObamaCare exchange cost taxpayer $120 million and only enrolled a few thousand consumers.[73] Washington, who has tried to comply with the ACA, nullified Obama's proposal to extend canceled policies, stating that they will not allow Obama's "fix to go through."[74] Sens. Mary Landrieu (D-La.) and Mark Udall (D-Colo.) introduced plans that would let people keep their plans even IF insurers cancel them. They want to look good for voters and the media, but Washington's response shows that even if insurers want to extend their plans, they may be unable to do so because of time constraints, state regulations, or state mandates.

Taxes

The Supreme Court ruled that the individual mandate was a tax. All persons must have government-approved health care insurance or pay a penalty tax. According to the U.S. Code, the penalty for individuals is below. The figures are a bit more complex for families. The United States Code is a consolidation and codification by subject matter of the general and permanent laws of the United States. The latest H.R. 3950 with the Amendments is different from what was codified in the U.S. Code. The table is based on the U.S. Code, yet according to H.R. 3950, the amount is supposed to be .5% for 2014, 1 % for 2015, and 2.0% beginning after 2015.[75] Title 26 concerns the IRS. It is unknown why there is a discrepancy in these penalty amounts.

Individual Mandate Penalty Table[76]

	Year 2014	Year 2015	Year 2016	After 2016
income based penalty	1% of income above filing threshold	2% of income above filing threshold	2.5% of income above filing threshold	2.5% of income above filing threshold
minimum penalty amount	$95	$325	$695	$695 + inflation adjustment

If an uninsured person complies by signing up with the state or federal exchange, this is a hefty percentage of one's income to participate. It is hard to figure out how much an individual or a family may be penalized, but Dr. Scott Gottlieb and his assistant ran the numbers for a non-smoking 30-year-old individual who chose an Aetna silver plan for various incomes in four different states.[77] These people pay between 11-45% of their gross income when yearly premiums and deductibles are taken into account. This does not include the additional amount that they pay for out of pocket expenses. Much of the cost of ObamaCare varies according to age, smoking, geography, insurance carrier, and plan type. So obtaining these numbers for comparison purposes is not an easy task.

	Arizona			Penn.		
Gross Yrly	Premium	Deductible	% income	Premium	Deductible	% income
20000	1716	600	0.1158	1620	600	0.111
25000	2424	4000	0.3212	2328	4000	0.3164
30000	2772	5000	0.3886	3108	5000	0.4054
35000	2772	5000	0.3886	3792	5000	0.4396
40000	2772	5000	0.3886	3792	5000	0.4396
45000	2772	5000	0.3886	3792	5000	0.4396
	Texas			Illinois		
	Premium	Deductible	% income	Premium	Deductible	% income
20000	1752	600	0.1176	2868	600	0.1734
25000	2460	4000	0.323	3576	4000	0.3788
30000	3240	5000	0.412	4092	5000	0.4546
35000	3336	5000	0.4168	4092	5000	0.4546
40000	3336	5000	0.4168	4092	5000	0.4546
45000	3336	5000	0.4168	4092	5000	0.4546

ObamaCare is about 50% funded by taxes and tax penalties.[78] Of that amount, tax penalties are expected to generate 5% of funding for ObamaCare.[79] As if the burden of these additional taxes of 11-45% onto what State and Federal taxes you are already paying isn't enough, there are many more taxes added to the list.

1. **Investment income** -Homeowner sales, unearned income interest, rental income, capital gains, and dividends - 3.8% surtax for individuals earning above $200,000 and married couples earning above $250,000.[80] John Kartch explains:

   > Under current law, the capital gains tax rate for all Americans rises from 15 to 20 percent in 2013, while the top dividend rate rises from 15 to 39.6 percent.

The new ObamaCare surtax takes the top capital gains rate to 23.8 percent and top dividend rate to 43.4 percent.[81]

2. **Federal Medicare hospital tax increases** - single Americans who earn above $200,000 per year (or $250,000 for couples) from 1.45% to 2.35%. (This increase will not go to fund Medicare.)[82]
3. **"Cadillac" health insurance** – up to 40% tax
4. **Medicare premiums** - Higher income means higher Part D premiums for those receiving Medicare.
5. **Pharmaceutical and Health Insurance Fees** passed onto consumers. These taxes include health insurance per number of enrollees ($2/enrollee)[83], medical devices (2.3%) and name brand drugs. The Joint Committee and the CBO confirm that this tax will cost the average family $300 to $400 dollars a year in added premium costs.[84]

   According to the New York Post:

   > Blue Cross Blue Shield of Alabama has a separate line item for "Affordable Care Act Fees and Taxes." The new taxes on one customer's bill added up to $23.14 a month, or $277.68 annually, according to Kaiser Health News. It boosted the monthly premium from $322.26 to $345.40 for that individual.
   >
   > The new taxes and fees include a 2 percent levy on every health plan.
   >
   > There's also a $2 fee per policy that goes into a new medical-research trust fund called the Patient Centered Outcomes Research Institute... [and] Insurers pay a 3.5 percent user fee to sell medical plans on the Health care.gov Web site.[85]

6. **Bracket creep** – when inflation drives taxpayers into a higher tax bracket.[86] The cumulative cost of inflation since 2009 is 9.4%.[87] Inflation is considered the hidden tax.

7. **The Flexible Spending Account (FSA) Cap of $2500** is "perhaps the most hurtful provision to the middle class."[88] These are pre-tax accounts that used to have no limit. People would use them for items like braces for children or tuition for special-needs children, costing much more than $2500.
8. **Medicine Cabinet tax** – Can no longer use HSA/FSA to cover non-prescription, over the counter medicine with pre-tax funds, except insulin.
9. **Medical itemized deduction** – Moved from 7.5% up to 10% threshold of adjusted gross income for those with out-of-pocket medical expenses.[89]
10. **Health Savings Account (HSA) Withdrawal Tax Hike**.[90] Increased from 10% up to 20%.
11. **Indoor Tanning Services Tax** - 10% excise tax on people using tanning salons.
12. **Elective Cosmetic Procedures** – 5%.[91]
13. **Black Liquor** – Biofuel tax increase.
14. **The small business tax credit** expires next year, 12/31/15.
15. **Employer Mandate** –

> "If an employer does not offer health coverage, and at least one employee qualifies for a health tax credit, the employer must pay an additional non-deductible tax of $2000 for all full-time employees. [This] applies to all employers with 50 or more employees. If any employee actually receives coverage through the exchange, the penalty on the employer for that employee rises to $3000. If the employer requires a waiting period to enroll in coverage of 30-60 days, there is a $400 tax per employee ($600 if the period is 60 days or longer).[92]"

Many businesses will either stop hiring people, cut back employee hours to under 30 hours a week (25% "tax" these people will be paying in lost wages) or drop health care and only pay the $2000 penalty. It is small wonder that Obama unilaterally moved the compliance date until after elections.

16. **Charitable Hospitals** – Hospitals helping the poor, will be fined $50,000 for failure to meet all the new DHHS regulations.
17. **Economic substance doctrine** expected to net $4.5 billion dollars - The IRS can disallow legal tax deductions by "deeming that the 'action lacks substance' and is merely intended to reduce taxes owed."[93]
18. **Exemptions – "**religious objectors, undocumented immigrants, prisoners, those earning less than the poverty line, members of Indian tribes, and hardship cases (determined by DHHS)."[94]

I agree with John C. Goodman that taxes need to be fair. Taxes do not need to be arbitrary, unfair and regressive.[95] He points out, that "only employer purchased health insurance receives favorable tax treatment." Moreover, the "amount of subsidy depends on your tax bracket. People who earn $100,000 a year get a tax subsidy that is six times the subsidy available to someone earning $25,000."[96]

> Families will be required to have health insurance - either through an employer, the government or in a newly created health insurance exchange. Take a family earning, say, $30,000. If the family qualifies for Medicaid, the government will pay 100% of the cost. If the family qualifies for insurance in the exchange, the government will pay about 95% of the cost. But if the family is eligible for insurance at work, the government subsidy will equal only 15% of the cost. Families at the same income level can receive subsidies that differ by $10,000 or even $20,000.[97]

Between all the Federal taxes and State taxes that people pay not only on wages, but on living expenses for the average person, the total is varied depending on income and personal choice – 30-60%.[98] Conservatively speaking, if the total tax percentage was only 30% and you add ObamaCare to it, people will be seeing between 40-80% of their income diminished in taxes. If you take the larger number, it is even more alarming to think that 70-90% of our income is spent on taxes. Unless we throttle the spending habits of the government, the taxes will only go up. Already taxes are at an unsustainable level such that a balanced budget and strict accounting for where the money is going is not too much for people to ask of their government. I'll bring this point up again in later sections.

Socialized Medicine – The Past and Present

Britain and Canada both have socialized medicine. Since much of what ObamaCare is trying to do is similar to what has happened in these two countries, it might help understand what ObamaCare is and what it is trying to accomplish.

We were told that ObamaCare would provide quality, affordable health care to all U.S. citizens. We were told that ObamaCare would be so good that all of the uninsured would now be insured. And we were told that we could keep our health insurance and our doctors. ObamaCare was such a good deal, that it would pay for itself and provide a $143 billion surplus to spend down the exponentially growing $17T deficit. What a deal! Or, is it really?

According to Sally Pipes, the Canadian system shows:

> Almost 700,000 people on waiting lists for surgery and other necessary treatments.[99]
>
> Wait times to see a specialist is about 16 weeks. With cancer or cardiac problems, would you or a loved one with cancer want to wait 4 months to see an oncologist or cardiologist? Now the wait times are 73% greater than in 1997.[100]
>
> When doctors are paid less, they go elsewhere and Canadian doctors are not an exception. In 1970, Canada had the fourth largest number of doctors per

thousand people out of a list of 30. Now they are ranked down at the bottom at 26th out of 30 countries.[101] Canadian doctors paid by the provincial government, earn 42 percent of what an American doctor earns.[102]

Even the Canadian Court in Quebec recognized that the public Canadian health care system had major problems. They upheld the right to seek private medical care, since patients in the public system often had to wait months to see a doctor, opting out of the public system and buying private insurance was often the only way to receive treatment in a timely manner.[103]

Canadians pay a lot of taxes to finance universal care, yet they still must pay out of pocket for some services.[104] About ¼ of chronically ill people surveyed said that "they had skipped their medications or neglected to fill a prescription because it was too expensive."[105]

Many Canadians travel to the United States and pay out of pocket for treatments and procedures, as they feel the wait in Canada is too long and harmful to their health.[106]

The UK has similar issues with their socialized medicine. Accordingly, the British system shows:

Every year, Britain's National Health Service (NHS) cancels around 100,000 operations. As of 2008, more than one million Britons were waiting for hospital admission.[107]

Each year more than 100,000 patients contract infections or illnesses that they didn't have before being admitted to NHS hospitals.[108] My guess is that only the sickest people are admitted and the cost-cutting measures kept people from getting timely treatment. There is probably less sterility because the hospital is directly incentivized to cut costs.

Britain has a government agency whose job it is to limit people's access to drugs.[109]

Britain recently had a scandal that NHS doctors were prematurely ending lives of thousands of elderly hospital patients.[110]

In Westcliff-on-Sea, an elderly woman was denied surgery because her travel distance from home left too large of a carbon footprint.[111]

For other countries with socialized medicine, there are some other issues that have sprung up:

There, some patients stuck on waiting lists have resorted to going to veterinarians, who operate in the private market and are in plentiful supply.[112]

Many Swedes go to neighboring countries for dental care, even though they've paid taxes for the service at home.[113]

Americans had some of the best health care in the world, prior to ObamaCare:

A 2008 study in Lancet Oncology found that, compared to Europeans and Canadians, Americans have a better survival rate—five years after diagnoses—for thirteen out of sixteen of the most common cancers.[114]

The survival rate among American women with breast cancer is 83.9 percent, while in Britain it's just 69.7 percent. For men with prostate cancer, the survival

> rate is 91.9 percent in the United States, 73.7 percent in France, and 51.1 percent in Britain.[115]
>
> Americans who don't die in homicides or car accidents outlive people in every other Western country.[116]

After Massachusetts enacted RomneyCare in 2006, "440,000 people have been added to the insurance rolls, including Medicaid or government-funded plans."[117] This forced doctors to quit, retire, or move out of state. Less doctors meant that people had problems finding a doctor.[118] One clinic in Western Massachusetts had a waiting list of 1,600 patients.[119] Romneycare cost the State almost 20,000 jobs, increased health insurance costs by more than $4 billion, lowered disposable income almost $400 per household, and leaving a family of four with the highest health care premiums in the nation.[120]

Even today, Danielle Kimberly in *Ebony* stated that when she signed up for ObamaCare, she had been rejected by 96 doctors trying to find one who would accept ObamaCare.[121] Since she made the statement as an avid supporter of Obama, the rejections did not dampen her spirits.

Breitbart News contributor Scot Vorse learned the hard way about ObamaCare's narrow networks when the nearest dentist who accepted the mandatory dental plan for his children was over 100 miles away.[122]

Medicaid is accepted by less than half of the doctors in the largest cities in the U.S.[123] Specialists are even harder to find:

> Only 7 percent of cardiologists in Minneapolis accept Medicaid; only 15 percent of dermatologists in Philadelphia; only 35 percent of obstetricians and gynecologists in Denver; only 28 percent of orthopedists in Seattle, and only 32 percent of family practitioners in New York City.[124]

Many people signed up for Medicaid who try to find a provider will find a bait and switch approach. There are few contracts for government care, so when one is located, it is most likely not accepting additional Medicaid patients. So, the patient can choose to go to the other, more expensive place if they agree to pay for out of pocket costs.[125]

In New Jersey, 1,800 middle class families received letters canceling their children's health plans.[126]

A man in Las Vegas signed up for United Health care under the ObamaCare exchange and he paid for the premium. A computer glitch is blamed for his triple bypass operation costing him $407,000.[127]

The scenario is that a married person with diabetes has a household income of $60,000. Her husband has insurance through his employer. She tried to sign up for ObamaCare in Washington State. She makes $11/hour. Her monthly premium is $400 with a deductible of $5,000. The monthly premium is 21% of her gross income, but with the deductible, it is 43% of her income. At this time, she is contemplating a divorce to be able to afford health care.

Cancer treatment is limited by ObamaCare. With the emphasis on cutting costs, the emphasis on quality cancer care is severely curtailed. The Associated Press survey found that "only four of 19 nationally recognized comprehensive cancer centers that responded to AP's survey said patients have access through all the insurance companies in their state exchange."[128] The survey also found that:

> Seattle Cancer Care Alliance is excluded by five out of eight insurers in Washington State's insurance exchange. MD Anderson Cancer Center says it's in less than half of the plans in the Houston area. Memorial Sloan-Kettering is included by two of nine insurers in New York City and has out-of-network agreements with two more.[129]

In New Jersey, despite signing up for ObamaCare, a couple was left with significant costs that were not covered by Horizon Blue Cross Blue Shield. Their insurance company only covered the lower costing, high co-pay procedures.[130]

A couple month ago, a document from the Department of Veterans Affairs linked dying veterans to the delays in VA hospitals. This study included 82 veterans who had died or were in the process of dying. One veteran who was suffering painful rectal bleeding reported having to wait a year for the earliest available colonoscopy appointment.[131]

In Washington, the website was erroneously debiting peoples' bank accounts.[132]

Betsy McCaughey states, "Foster predicts that unless these cuts are repealed, about 15% of hospitals will be forced into the red. Others will be forced to operate in an environment of scarcity, with fewer nurses on the floor, fewer cleaners, longer waits for high-tech diagnostic tests. That will affect all patients."[133]

A woman who asked the question – Would you deny my 96-year-old grandmother a pacemaker? She didn't get a real answer.

The UK is now realizing that socialized medicine is too expensive (18% of their budget), too inefficient, and too full of bureaucracy to serve people in a timely fashion.[134] The UK is now in the process of partially privatizing the National Health Service (NHS) to avoid a financial meltdown like what happened in Greece. David Cameron says, "If we were as good at treating cancer as the average European country, we would save 5,000 lives a year."[135] At present and under the best of circumstances, those with heart disease or cancer will wait more than 5-1/2 months to be treated.[136]

Last November, such rationing reached a scandalous level. A study by the Co-operation and Competition Panel (CCP) revealed that Primary Care Trust (PCT) heads were imposing arbitrary spending caps, denying patients treatment for procedures such as hip replacements and cataract removals–and that waiting times for services were being deliberately extended "so that patients would go private or die before they were seen" to slash costs."[137]

"So why would we continue to pursue such an approach to health care, even as the latest cautionary tale from the European Union emerges? Sally Pipes, an American health policy expert who leads the Pacific Research Institute in San Francisco put it best. "They [President Barack Obama, Senate Majority Leader Harry Reid, and House Minority Leader Nancy Pelosi] are ideologues," said Pipes. "They don't care whether the system really works or not. They have an ideological goal in mind." One this troika seems doggedly determined to pursue, even if it drives the country bankrupt in the process."[138]

I've covered the history of socialized medicine from Britain and Canada, and then looked at the state of U.S. medicine prior to ObamaCare. RomneyCare as a precursor to ObamaCare was discussed, and finally what we are just now starting to see with the implementation of ObamaCare. I have also included the aftermath for the UK. They are in the process of going back to privatization of health care to help control costs.

ObamaCare promised that it would only cut costs and not cut any benefits. These types of issues are inexcusable in the greatest nation in the world. I wish I could say they were isolated incidents, but the more people who try to use socialized medicine or ObamaCare realize just how poor the care really is. There is a lot of misrepresentation going on. People believe ObamaCare health insurance covers them for costly procedures, when it doesn't. Or patients don't realize how much deductibles and out of pocket costs they will be paying in addition to their monthly premium. Just like participants in Romneycare found out, there would be increased health care premiums, longer waits to see a doctor or receive life-saving care, poorer care, health care rationing, and there will be declining effects on employment and household income. It looks like the public reasons for passing ObamaCare were wrong. Declining benefits are part of the reality.

Exchanges

There are two places to buy ObamaCare health insurance, either at a state exchange or at a federal exchange. Theoretically, those working for small businesses and who could not afford private health insurance, could now get affordable health care coverage. When health insurance is no longer tied to employment, it also gives employees more job flexibility to change jobs or work on their own.

Raul Labrador, a Congressman from Idaho, wrote his constituency a letter. In that letter, he details a House Oversight and Government Reform Committee hearing on health insurance exchanges. There are some clear differences between a state created exchange and a federally created exchange within the state. For instance, a true state exchange would tailor its options to the needs of its residents. Yet, because of the ObamaCare mandate and the amount of money flowing through the state exchanges, "when the feds control the money, they control the product."

Moreover, it is not a state exchange when it has to get federal approval prior to allowing money to flow through a state system. In essence, if the federal government has the power to impose their will on a state exchange, they could just as easily and arbitrarily impose their will on an exchange created through ObamaCare.[139] According to Michael Cannon, Director of Health Policy Studies at the non-partisan Cato Institute, "if you want a federal government to control the state, then the best thing you can do is establish an exchange."

Many states have opted out of participating in the exchanges. According to section 1321 of the ACA, if a state does not set up an exchange or sets up an exchange that fails to meet federal standards by January 2013, then the federal government will come into the state to set up an exchange. This part of the law was ruled unconstitutional by the Supreme Court because the federal government could not hold Medicare hostage to force the states to comply with ObamaCare. However, this section also fails constitutionality because whoever controls the health care in a state will control the state. That would destroy the sovereignty of States guaranteed under the 10th Amendment.

Then again, because of funding issues, Cannon, went on to say in the hearing, "If the state does not establish an exchange then there might not be an exchange at all because we all know there is no funding to create these exchanges, and it's not likely that Congress is going to approve [any]."

There is a $2,000 per employee penalty levied on employers who live in exchange states. Cannon affirmed that penalties against employers "would not apply in a state that does not create its own Exchange."

As discussed in the Agency section above, there is an issue with tax treatment of subsidies if a person enrolls in ObamaCare under a federally established exchange. The law says that the subsidies can only be given to a state exchange. The IRS said that there was a drafting mistake by Congress but the law really means that citizens signing up for any exchange is entitled to the premium subsidies. This means that the IRS has been offering tax incentives to citizens in all 50 states despite the Supreme Court ruling that bars federal control over any states who opt out of participation in ObamaCare.

A lot of money has been wasted on developing websites to interface with consumers. The federal exchange website cost almost $400 million.[140] Maryland spent $90 million before announcing it would start over and use Connecticut's model for their exchange.[141] They will try to get some of the money back mainly from Noridian Health Care Solutions, but also intend to ask for more grant money.[142] Oregon spent

$130 million for a non-functional website and enrolled 69,000 people via paper applications.[143] Now, Nevada has dumped its exchange. Unsurprisingly, California is far over budget. Massachusetts does not have functioning websites yet. Hawaii spent $204 million to sign up 8,000 people. Vermont, one of the smallest states was awarded $168 million by the government to set up their exchange.

Setting up health insurance through ObamaCare exchanges has some monumental issues. These issues range from unconstitutionality, to agencies going outside of their delegation of power, to outright wasting a lot of taxpayer money. For the federal government to buy off States with the lure of a lot of money effectively transfers the power of a State to the Federal government. The health care budget is so large and many States need money from any source to avoid bankruptcy.

Enrollment

Section 3021 of the ACA is about health information technology, enrollment standards, and protocols. The reason that enrollment is such a big deal is that it is crucial for the survival of ObamaCare that the right mix of people enroll in the government health care system. Another issue regarding enrollment is the employees that are hired to enroll people in the exchanges. Many have questionable backgrounds to be handling such a vast amount of sensitive information. A third issue is the federal website regarding security and functionality of the website. A fourth issue is the sharing of private information between the federal government and the state governments.

In order to enroll, the person must be uninsured, or in the process of buying their own insurance, not eligible for Medicaid or affordable employer coverage, and residing in the country legally.

The insurances are looking for a larger number of healthy people to pay premiums. Ideally, these are people who have very little need for health care so that their money will pay for the sicker, more costly people. That way the health insurances do not lose a lot of money. The individual mandate that everyone must be insured or face a penalty speaks to the serious need for this funding source. The current projection by the Congressional Budget Office is that 40% or 2.8 million people need to be the young invincibles (healthy and 18-34 years old). The next largest category are adults ages 35-54 are projected at 37% of the mix. If the young invincibles fail to sign up, then insurance will raise premiums for everyone else in the program.

The government did a preliminary study on how many previously uninsured people from the ages of 18-64 would not sign up for ObamaCare. A full 50% said they would not sign up, meaning that the government knows that 5 million of these people will not be paying premiums, but instead will be subjected to the IRS penalties.[144]

One interesting part of section 3021 talks about when a person enrolls in ObamaCare, there is an electronic match against existing federal and state data that includes vital records, employment history, enrollment systems and tax records. Right now, I don't believe that most state records are shared with the federal government, but when you sign up for ObamaCare, both the state and federal records are crosschecked.

It would be refreshing to see a part of ObamaCare that was really meant to help people without being political about it. Unfortunately, enrollment comes with voter registrations pre-marked as "Democrat."[145] California justified this through a statute that gives state offices the authority to provide services to persons with disabilities.[146] This includes giving them a voter registration form and "assistance in completing the form." Since she made the statement as an avid supporter of Obama, the rejections did not dampen her spirits.

In the beginning, I mentioned that the U.S. had about 10 million people who were uninsured and without access to health care. This was the justification the government gave for national health care. The enrollment figures should be measured against this group to show how effective the legislation is. There needs to be questions such as, "Does the ACA meet its stated goals?" There are several problems with the way the numbers are being told to the public because the numbers are mixing apples and oranges. There is no direct way to measure the target group effectively.

Insurances don't count people as insured unless they pay the premium, so neither should those keeping track of ObamaCare enrollments. The government made a big push for an enrollment of 7 million. Magically, there were 7.1 million people signed up at the deadline for enrollment. Later the number changed to 8 million enrollees. There were no official numbers for how many people were previously uninsured, how many were dumped into the system by insurances cancelling their policies, or how many of these were the coveted young invincibles. However, it was estimated from several independent studies that the previously uninsured population signing up for ObamaCare was between 1.6 and 2.1 million.[147] Additionally, it was estimated that around 28% of those were in the young invincible category.[148]

Georgia provides us with some actual numbers, but whether they are representative of the rest of the country, time will tell. Georgia estimated that they had 650,000 people who were eligible for subsidies through the health exchange. Of those, they received around 220,000 applications, of which about 49% of those applications paid their premiums.[149] The applications covered 149,465 Georgians, yet the Georgia insurance department estimated that about 400,000 of their people would lose insurance due to the new coverage mandates.[150]

As of May 3, 2014, the House Committee released new numbers. There were 5.36 million who paid for their policies. Earlier I had mentioned that 40% needed to be from the age category of 18-34. The new figures show 25% in that age bracket. Ages 35-54 needs to be 37% for the correct mix to make ObamaCare successful. The numbers show 39% in that category. According to the subsequent House Committee numbers, enrollment was a large failure. It failed to attract the healthy people it needed and failed abysmally at insuring the previously uninsured.

The federal ObamaCare website is a "mess" and "missing huge, critical pieces."[151] According to Heather Ginsberg, one major part of Healthcare.gov that is still not working properly is the "function that accurately pays insurers."[152] The government should be able to track how many people signed up, what their premium is, if they have paid that premium, and how many applications did not go through. The government claims that the website is 100% secure. Many legitimate hackers working for internet security companies say otherwise.

During a Senate Judiciary hearing last year, former Health and Human Services Secretary Kathleen Sebelius admitted ObamaCare navigators could be felons.[153] In California alone, at least 43 convicted criminals have worked as navigators and handling sensitive information of private citizens. People who used to belong to ACORN, a group that lost federal funding in 2009 for alleged illegal activity like promoting underage prostitution and tax fraud, have been brought in to run ObamaCare navigator programs. There was such a push to get 7 million people to sign up for ObamaCare, I saw a video with a navigator telling an enrollee to lie so their premium would be smaller. Project Veritas caught navigators in Dallas telling people to lie about their income or their smoking status to get higher subsidies, lower premiums and avoid being audited by the IRS.[154]

Rep. Darrell Issa released a report from the House Committee on Oversight and Government Reform in December 2013 that detailed disturbing issues regarding the navigator and assister program. One preliminary report stated that "lax Navigator and Assister training requirements and vague marketing standards increased the likelihood of identity theft for consumers"[155] The poor training was directly responsible for giving incorrect information about the exchanges and violations of DHHS rules and procedures.

Because the navigator program does not have background checks, and some people they hire are untrustworthy, there is a lot of potential for fraud and criminal activity.[156]

There is a lot of focus on enrollment because these numbers represent how much confidence the American public has in government-run health care. But there are many issues regarding fudging of the enrollment numbers to support a political agenda, security and functionality of the federal ObamaCare website, big media misinformation, navigator problems, and private information sharing between the federal government and the states.

Enforcement

Enforcement of a congressional law is usually through an executive branch agency that is delegated that particular power. In the ACA, that designation appropriately falls to the Internal Revenue Service especially since the Supreme Court ruled that the individual mandate is a tax. The law specifically states that noncompliance is not a criminal offense. Although enforcement is through the IRS, the only power they have is through assessment of fines and collection from offsets of any IRS tax refunds. The IRS cannot put a lien on property or put people in jail. So far, that is all the law specifically allows for enforcement.

ObamaCare provides as much as $10 billion dollars for the IRS to upgrade their system to implement enforcement of the ACA mandates. At last count, the IRS was looking for 6500 new agents, or 130 new agents per state.[157] Unfortunately, there will be a significant increase in the number of criminal investigators. Their job is to increase financial penalties whenever possible.[158] Since the IRS has steadily disregarded Congressional boundaries, I would expect abuse in many of the enforcement gray areas. For instance, the IRS interpreted that Congress made a drafting mistake in the ACA and as such, the IRS illegally gives subsidies to all enrollees in all 50 states. (See Agency discussion of the IRS above) One blurred line could be between what is specifically allowed by Congress and the IRS policy of turning debts over to private collection agencies who currently collect 25 cents per every dollar they collect and a $100 for every account they close.[159]

The problem is that once something like this is in place, Congress (and apparently the IRS) can now change enforcement protocols without the public scrutiny that was given to the ACA. I shudder to think why IRS agents are being trained with semi-automatic rifles and handguns.[160] Whether or not enforcement will expand to include labor camps or liens on private property remains to be seen.

Waivers & Exemptions

Throughout the ACA, there are numerous sections that grant the Secretary of DHHS the power to grant waivers of any or all portions of sections to applicants. On one hand, the waivers were meant to stabilize the system during the transition time until full implementation of the ACA. On the other hand, some say that the waivers were politically motivated since there was no objective criteria to determine who got a waiver and who didn't.[161]

Waivers and exemptions serve the same function – to allow for non-compliance with the law in one or more aspects. The difference between a waiver and an exemption seems to be that waivers are temporary with most granted until 2014 or until they can use an exemption.[162] Exemptions are for a longer period, but may require periodic review. DHHS granted 1231 to 1625 waivers covering about 3.1 to 4 million people depending on the source.[163] Of those waivers about one-third to one-half of them were granted to unions.[164]

Congress specifically did not exempt themselves in the law, contrary to what many people may think. The ACA says that Congress and their staff would lose their current health coverage and it imposed a $5,000 to $11,000 pay cut.[165] Yet, like so many laws, this one was not enforced. Not only did they keep their current health plans[166], but the Office of Personnel Management proposed a rule that the federal government could continue to contribute to health care premiums.[167] Consequently, any pay cut Congress might have voted themselves is now a net wash with the money going to pay their premiums for health care instead of part of their salary.

There are other individual exemptions or waivers from the individual mandate. These are: 1) for a religious conscience[168]; 2) if you are a member of a 'health care sharing ministry;" 3) immigration status (illegally in the country); 4) a Member of an Indian tribe; or 5) "Hardship based" according to the IRS code[169] which also includes people who fall below a certain income level, and 6) if under age 26, a person can be covered as a dependent on their parent's health insurance.

After the public outcry from losing their health care insurance, the government declared that those who lost their insurance and couldn't afford the new premiums would qualify for the hardship exemption. Those who consider "other available policies unaffordable" also fall under the hardship exemption. Theoretically, people can get a hardship exemption for unspecified reasons, which requires "documentation if possible."[170]

Another type of waiver is one that allows purchase of barebones health insurance, otherwise known as catastrophic coverage plans. This waiver is available for people under 30 years of age. After 500,000 people started having their policies cancelled because the insurance did not offer federally compliant health care, then the government expanded this waiver to all ages.[171] I am unclear if this expansion is only for people who lost their insurance or if it is for everyone. But, like Sen Marco Rubio stated, this backpedaling and offering cheaper insurance as another Band-Aid fix is "a slap in the face to the thousands of Americans who have already purchased expensive insurance through the ObamaCare exchanges."[172]

Discrimination

Unfortunately, discrimination is a loaded word, much like "racism." However, discrimination is a legal term that ties into constitutionally protected civil rights. There are three tier judicial tests as to whether the government treats similarly situated citizens differently. If it is a constitutionally protected right such as discrimination against religion, race, or privacy, then the court applies a strict scrutiny standard to determine if the law is discriminatory. If the law is gender-based discrimination, it falls under intermediate scrutiny. If the discrimination falls under any other type of category, then it is a rational basis test. This means the government has to have a rational basis for discriminating and is so broad that just about everything else can be justified under this test.

On its face, ObamaCare allows discrimination in three rational basis instances: 1) age, 2) smoking, and 3) geographic location. These distinctions provide the basis for calculating health care premiums. ObamaCare discriminates in its effect according to physical ailments, pre-existing medical care, and income. Since race and ethnicity can be a source of discrimination, I included immigration status in this section too.

Age

Age discrimination involves treating someone differently because of his or her age. As yet, there have been no constitutional challenges for age, but I think there could be several grounds for a lawsuit linked to the treatment of seniors through Medicare as opposed to the general public on Medicaid. This is especially true since the government has asserted additional control over both programs and seniors covered by Medicare have been and will be hit the hardest with cuts. Medicare is subjected to the Independent Payment Advisory Board (IPAB) actions outside the control of Congress. I'll discuss Medicare and the IPAB further below in sections called "Medicare" and "Independent Payment Advisory Board (IPAB)" respectively.

Children up to age 26 can be covered under their parent's policies. People up to age 30 can be eligible to carry only catastrophic insurance, which makes their monthly premiums much less than a normal plan and it will pay up to

60% of the medical expenses. I don't know how much the deductible is, but high deductibles plague the regular plans. Premiums for older people cannot be more than three times as much than for younger people.[173]

The young invincibles are the age group of 26 to 34 year olds who pay for the individual mandate, but who will not be using health care much, if at all.[174] The system needs 40% of these people in the insurance mix to be cost effective. Do you know that unmarried males ages 21-34 go to the doctor an average of 6 times in 13 years?[175] When these people pay hundreds a month for insurance with $5,000 deductibles, this really doesn't seem fair for an age group already plagued with high unemployment, inflation, and higher costs of living. Not only are the youngsters paying for something they rarely use, but their money is being used to fund the sicker, more costly people. The other issue is that these people will be in the system the longest so they will presumably pay a much higher percentage of the total health care cost and indebtedness over their lifetime that is caused from ObamaCare.

Senior citizens, who are enrolled in Medicare, will be denied care simply based on their age. Age will be a large factor in determining whether it is cost effective to give a senior a pacemaker, heart surgery, or cancer treatment. Instead, seniors can look forward to mandatory death counselling is to help motivate them to die. Their medicine and care is rationed through decisions from the IPAB, increased bureaucracy, and less privacy protection. They will have longer waiting lines due to the increased number of people added to the doctor rolls, and while Medicare premiums increase, there will be fewer benefits available.

Evidence from studies in California and Pennsylvania are scary and should provide a cautionary tale for the care of seniors. "Seniors with pneumonia, congestive heart failure, stroke and hip fractures were more likely to die from these conditions in the low spending hospitals than in the high spending hospitals."[176] Moreover, the study concluded, "13,815 California seniors treated at low spending hospitals would have survived and left the hospital had they received more care."[177] Pennsylvania came to similar conclusions. Since the IAPB and ObamaCare both provide for significantly lowered payments to hospitals and for medical costs, who will protect our seniors?

ObamaCare is written with the underlying assumption that seniors provide the largest financial drain on the medical system. As such, to reduce costs, Medicare is specifically targeted. Another erroneous assumption is that because the public overuses specialists, that there is a need to shift patients towards their primary care doctors because they cost less than specialists. In the U.S., about five percent of the populace needs 50% of the care.[178] While this population includes seniors, it isn't all seniors. Both of the above assumptions are faulty and can be corrected to save a lot of money.

According to Betsy McCaughey, "health care costs for seniors are increasing far more slowly than the rest of the population."[179] The focus of senior health care should be in keeping them from becoming disabled. When a senior becomes disabled, they cost seven times more than if they were not disabled.[180] Furthermore, she says, "Surgeries to unclog arteries, replace worn out hips and knees, and remove cataracts have had a major impact on achieving steadily declining disability rates."[181] Medical research shows that primary care doctors are more likely to misdiagnose and treat the ailment incorrectly, causing more hospital admissions and patients dying sooner.[182]

Using heart specialists and cancer specialists can make sure that diagnosis are accurate, obtained in a timely fashion to avoid life-threatening wait times, and can prevent disease from progressing and becoming more expensive to treat.

Under section 4202 of the ACA, it deals with people from the ages of 55-64. This section provides grant money for 5-year pilot programs concerning public health community interventions, screenings and clinical referrals. Funding from this source could set up senior health clinics specific to keeping an elderly population from being disabled.

CLASS represents the ObamaCare wish list for a long-term care solution. Consistent with this administration, it was discontinued because it was not financially feasible. According to Dan Weber, President of the Association of Mature American Citizens, on January 1, 2014, $22 billion dollars, representing 14% of the budget, was cut from the home health care services for seniors ages 60 and above.[183]

Since more and more people are living longer, age should be a celebration of life and there is no reason that our seniors cannot lead long and prosperous lives. With some proper precautionary screenings and follow-up care as needed, they will not be disabled and can be productive in society.

Right now, seniors and the young invincibles are paying the brunt of ObamaCare health insurance costs. The democrat/liberal mantra that ObamaCare only cuts costs, not benefits rings hollow, especially since the senior benefits carry a disproportionate share of the cost cutting. I will explain more in depth about aging issues under the IAPB section and the Medicare section below.

Where you live

Geographically, a person's premium cost differs as to whether a person lives in the city or in the rural area of a state. ObamaCare bureaucrats determined that those with a high cost of living could be charged more.[184]

Technically, ObamaCare health insurance is a national plan, so everyone should pay the same regardless of where they live. The reality is that some states are more subsidized or politicized than others and there can be up to a 50% difference in rates depending on where the enrollee lives. For instance, the Heritage Foundation compared insurance rates for 27 year olds across the country. They found that in red states (conservative states) the invincible's insurance rates went up 78%, while in blue states (liberal states) who supported Obama their insurance rates were increased by 50%.[185]

Physical Ailments

There are several ailments that do not fit into the one-size-fits-all ObamaCare health insurance. This includes diagnosis and treatment of cancer and heart disease. While health care insurance cannot deny anyone with pre-existing conditions, it doesn't mean they won't pay more than average people will. Disturbingly, ObamaCare specifically singles out people with diabetes, obesity, and high blood pressure.

Cancer & Heart Issues

Because cancer can be so expensive to treat, ObamaCare automatically imposes cost-cutting measures directly onto cancer patients, with most of those people between the ages of 50 to 60 years old. The same goes for people with cardiac issues. People's lives are turned into a cost/benefit analysis, which not only takes into account how expensive the treatment will be, but also the age of the person. That means an 80 year old with cancer would get death counselling, but a person who is much younger would be treated.

Not only does the system itself regulate which treatment options will be paid for, but there are issues of how much is covered under ObamaCare and also which hospitals and doctors will accept patients for treatments. According to the Associated Press, "just 4 of 19 nationally recognized comprehensive cancer centers offer ObamaCare access through all insurance plans in their state ObamaCare exchanges, and a McKinsey and Co. study revealed 38% of all ObamaCare plans only allow patients to pick from just 30% of the largest 20 hospitals in their areas."[186] Many plans exclude specialty cancer hospitals and many of the top cancer centers are not opting in to take such low payment and high regulation for their services.[187] That leaves fewer doctors and hospitals in the system that treat cancer.

A couple justifications for passing ObamaCare was that it was affordable and it would keep people from having to declare bankruptcy for medical bills. A New York man selected the gold Horizon BlueCross BlueShield Plan because he was facing cancer surgery. It was the highest plan with the lowest deductible that would allow him to maintain access to his cancer doctors. The only coverage BlueCross allowed was for lower-costing, high co-pay procedures.[188] The couple had a mountain of debt that they will probably have to file bankruptcy for. Another story was a Las Vegas man who was left with a $407,000 bill under ObamaCare through United Health Care.[189]

Another story involving government-run health care involves the Veteran's Administration in Washington State and in Phoenix, Arizona, killing veterans through denying appropriate, timely access to medical care. These are real stories that don't go away just because someone wants to label them "anti-ObamaCare misinformation." What happened to those Veterans is at best total incompetence and at worse pure evil. If it can happen to Veterans, it can happen to those receiving Medicare or Medicaid under government-run ObamaCare.

Chronic Conditions

Section 2703 addresses a state option to provide health homes for enrollees with chronic conditions. Specifically labeled as chronic conditions are: 1) mental health conditions, 2) substance abuse, 3) asthma, 4) diabetes, 5) heart disease, and 6) obesity. There is no mention of cancer as being a chronic health condition, yet lumping these six items together doesn't seem to make a lot of sense. Many people with these listed ailments do get better and do not remain in a chronically ill situation. Moreover, in section 10410, they provide for "Centers of Excellence for Depression." The definition of depression in section 520B is a "brain or mental disorder including major depression, bipolar disorder and related mood disorders." Who determines what are "related mood disorders"? Are we talking about women with PMS? Why would a chronic illness such as depression be singled out for a center of excellence, yet also be hidden in a global label of "mental health condition?" On the other hand, why don't the other chronic conditions get a center of excellence too?

This section might be good for some people, but whoever drafted this section had a larger vision because this singling out and labeling of certain chronic conditions but not others is downright spooky. For instance, now can they use this section for funding and control of mentally challenged individuals? Does use of the service automatically get reported on a gun registry for mental illness. And who decides to put these people in the home? Is it voluntary or involuntary? Do they round up all the obese people and put them in one place, such as one of those labor camps? I don't know. I just find that these sections have a lot of potential for abuse, especially when most of ObamaCare regulations are left to the discretion of Secretary of DHHS. I can tell you that there are wide nets of reports, data collection, and informational sharing between a lot of government agencies and contractors. My other concern is that any program the government deems as voluntary can become compulsory like the IRS or Social Security.

Pre-existing Medical Conditions

One of the carrots ObamaCare used was that health insurance could no longer deny people with pre-existing conditions. Money set aside for the temporary high-risk pool did not last long. The Center for Studying Health System Change found that 5.6 to 7 million people enrolling in ObamaCare would have pre-existing conditions, yet only enough money to cover about 200,000 people annually. [190] That study was wrong because the funding only lasted a little over a year.

Employer Wellness Programs

A potential backdoor way of discriminating comes through employer-mandated wellness programs. Much like New York's reaction to banning certain sizes of sugar-containing drinks comes the employer wellness programs. Employers and employees get certain incentives for instituting and participating in workplace wellness programs that are "reasonably designed" to promote health and prevent disease. Failure to participate in the wellness program or meet certain criteria (such as a weight goal), can subject an employee to company fines of up to 30% of their health care premium. Consider CVS drug stores levy a fine of $50/month or $600/year for employees who refuse to disclose their weight or other health measurements.[191] Walmart penalizes smokers by up to $2300 a year, yet ObamaCare allows employers to charge the employee 50% of the premium that they pay.[192]

There are potential privacy issues that go directly to your employer and potentially to everyone who has access to your federal medical file. For instance:

> Union leader Borsos also argues wellness plans can be very intrusive, asking a series of very personal questions. He pointed to one wellness plan, for instance, that asks such questions as "Have you ever had a total hysterectomy? How much do you weigh? In the last month, have you ever felt nervous or stressed? In the last month, how often have you been angered because of things beyond your control? During the past week, I have felt lonely-- yes or no? During the past week, I have felt sad, yes or no?"[193]

While there have been some additional employee protections regarding health-contingent wellness programs, the potential for abuse is still there.

Income

ObamaCare was sold to the public as a way for everyone to have affordable health care. They also pronounced that the rich would be paying more than their fair share through various taxes on the "rich." But what the public wasn't told is who was defined as rich. In actuality, the rich turned out to be the upper middle class. The reality is that the poor have always had medical care in one form or another. The rich can afford to pay for their medical care or for concierge medicine. That leaves the middle class holding the financial bag.[194]

There was an interesting report from Unite Here, a 300,000-member union that concludes that ObamaCare worsens income inequality by prompting businesses to cut back worker hours and offering incentives for businesses to dump their employees into the ObamaCare system.[195] It is like levying a 25% tax on these people by having their hours reduced from 40 to 30 hours, which is the federal definition of full-time. An unintended consequence is that ObamaCare fines businesses if any of their workers receives subsidized coverage through an exchange. Consequently, hiring decisions will be skewed in favor of upper-income neighborhoods because these people are less likely to qualify for subsidized insurance in the exchanges.

Immigration/Race/Ethnicity

Out of the many types of classifications that disparities can be viewed under, the Action Plan released by the Obama administration sets a target on only race and ethnicity.[196] As such, a lot of ObamaCare is aimed at minorities and minority medical services. For instance, the ACA creates or revises national student loans to require that low-income minority medical students must serve in their home communities if the area is designated as medically underserved.[197] I'm not sure it is doing minorities a favor to tell them if they accept student loans that they need to return to the Bronx, Watts, or a big city ghetto, if the government designates these areas as medically underserved.

A Gallup poll found that the "biggest insurance gains were among lower-income people and among African Americans."[198] On the other hand, "Latinos remained more likely than any other racial or ethnic group to lack access to care with 37% uninsured."[199] Although it may look like much of ObamaCare helps minorities, the more the government regulates what minorities can and can't do with their health, the more these programs are likely to reduce privacy, increase bureaucracy, and increase the risk of being designated as "at-risk" for whatever intervention the government wants to impose on them. Being designated as "at-risk" usually means that government workers have the authority to come into your home and designate how you will live your life, care for your children, and how or when you can use your government benefits. Obama himself was saying that if you couldn't afford ObamaCare, then you needed to re-prioritize your budget and cancel your cellphone. When will that kind of thinking become a law?

There are also several issues with ObamaCare immigration status. People who emigrate legally from another country are immediately eligible for ObamaCare. This is interesting because as Betsy McCaughey points out, legal immigrants are "not eligible for Medicaid for their first five years in the United States."[200]

As usual, the United Nations has publically been denouncing the United States, without a clue to the facts. This time it is for human rights concerns about illegal aliens not being included in ObamaCare.[201] Although illegal immigrants are not directly eligible for ObamaCare, they can still obtain care at the community health centers. The ACA allocates $11 billion dollars to the community health centers.[202]

Oregon "accidentally" enrolled 4,000 illegal immigrants into ObamaCare so that they wouldn't put a drain on the state Medicaid program.[203] The government actually went so far as to promise families with "illegal alien relatives that nobody would be deported for seeking ObamaCare services."[204]

I really hate to see ObamaCare single out minorities for special treatment and in the same breath equating them with being poor. I know many people who are minorities who are decent, hard-working people; race has no bearing on how or why they are part of the middle class or the rich. In these discussions, people of Asian origin are never mentioned as doing better than Caucasians, but as a group, they are.

Unfortunately, we are seeing class warfare tactics used on our own people. The real reason to single out people by race has to do with keeping people splintered and polarized so that they cannot unite against bad government policies of total control and destruction of constitutional rights so they can turn us into the Socialized States of America.

Cost-Shifting

Whenever insurance is involved, the goal is to shift costs. Two obvious ways of cost shifting are using the young invincible payments to pay for senior Medicare costs. The rich also subsidize the poor.

Everyone in ObamaCare subsidizes the insurance because insurance premiums can be adjusted upwards almost without ceilings. The only control on premiums is if Congress or DHHS decides that a particular insurance's increase was unwarranted and they kick them out of the exchange. But then again, if they do kick a compliant health insurance company out of the exchange, the repercussions could be extremely harmful to the insurees trying to find another insurance and doctors who will accept that particular insurance. The system is stacked up in favor of letting the premiums continue to rise unabated.

There is a lot of cost-shifting happening with ObamaCare. For instance, the health care bill shifted the cost of underwater retiree health care plans to the taxpayers by allocating resources under a section 1102 of the ACA called "Reinsurance for Early Retirees." The provision states that it is to reimburse employers for early retirement health care costs incurred for retirees not eligible for Medicare, but who are 55 or over. According to the Pew Foundation, 20 states have only paid in 7.1% to fund their retiree health care plans for their public employees.[205] A list of who was granted funding for the $5 billion dollar bailout is contained in Appendix D.

One of the larger costs in a state budget is funding for penitentiaries. Up to 35% of people enrolling in ObamaCare have been or are currently in prison.[206] Although prison inmates are not covered for standard health care, it does pay for hospital stays over 24 hours.[207] That means states can transfer millions of dollars of hospital care debt to the federal government. The other reason is that when the prisoners get out of jail, they have medical access for mental and addictive disorders, which the prison population has a disproportionately high percentage of than the normal public.[208]

Businesses are cost shifting to the public. With a fine of $3,000 per employee for businesses with over 49 full-time employees, businesses have started to cost-shift health insurance to the public since the fine can be lower than providing health care benefits. According to Guy Benson, quoting a Kaiser Health News report, "Since most big corporations are self-insured, shifting even one high-cost member out of the company plan could save the employer hundreds of thousands of dollars a year—while increasing the cost of claims absorbed by the marketplace policy by a similar amount."[209] This concern was raised in 2011, but is now being realized in 2014. Targeted dumping usually includes those people who cost the company the most to insure, which are the older and sicker employees.

According to Sally Pipes, "Medicaid shifted $16.2 billion in hospital costs (in 2006) and $23.7 billion in physician costs (in 2007) directly onto private payers. That means that Medicaid paid $39.9 billion less than it would have if all payers paid equivalent rates. If there was no cost-shift, private payments to hospitals and physicians would have been 15 percent lower." The numbers show that a family of four will pay $1,512 annually or 10.6 percent more from this cost-shifting.[210]

Another type of cost-shifting was designed so the public didn't realize the true cost of ObamaCare. The tax credits and subsidies hide the effect of the premium hikes that individuals will face until after the 2014 elections.[211]

ObamaCare isn't properly funded. The numbers change depending on who runs them. It is a little like robbing Peter to pay Paul when we have such a high national debt. For instance, $716 billion was cut from Medicare in order to help fund $1.9 trillion in new health care spending, through the law's expansion of Medicaid and newly subsidized exchanges.[212] But this time, the legislation went overboard by compelling everyone to participate in paying for a few people to gain control over national health care. It seems like ObamaCare is a deliberate attempt to pay the schemers and at the same time covertly reduce unfunded liabilities from other national problems like the Medicare and the Social Security system. By covertly, I mean that the reduction is not done publicly so it won't be reported by media and affect the way people vote in November.

Medicare

Medicare was enacted in 1965 as part of Social Security. According to Dr. Elaina George, Medicare and ObamaCare have several parallels:

- Just like ObamaCare, it was initially sold to Americans as a government program that would 'take care' of Americans. It would make the Government the benefactor, the caregiver, and the savior absolving Americans from personal responsibility – all you would have to do is put your faith and money in the government and everything would be taken care of with nothing to worry about.
- Just like ObamaCare, Medicare was drafted by bureaucrats and politicians who were more interested in concentrating power and controlling the purse strings, not providing true health care.
- Just like ObamaCare, there were no doctors or patients involved with the crafting of the legislation; and therefore, there was no one who was a true advocate for the patient.[213]

Actual costs were far larger than presented to people. The predicted cost for Medicare Part A was $9 billion in 1990. The actual cost for hospital insurance was $67 billion.[214] For the entire Medicare program, it was estimated that it would cost $12 billion in 1990. The actual cost was $110 billion.[215] The actual cost of Medicare today is an unfunded liability of $13 trillion dollars.[216] All together between Medicare, Medicaid, and Social Security the unfunded liabilities are estimated at around $88 trillion dollars.[217] Currently the big three programs account for 48% of government spending.[218] "Unfunded liabilities" is a fancy way to say that the money is not there, the program is underwater, and going bankrupt. ObamaCare was predicted to cost between $1 trillion and $2 trillion. Judging from the other numbers for sweeping national medical programs, ObamaCare will cost exponentially more than projected.

Medicare is one of the white elephants in the middle of the room and it is also a very sensitive voting issue. What the government is trying to do is to reduce Medicare spending without losing senior votes. They buried the Medicare reform in ObamaCare regulations, while continuing to tell seniors that everything is o.k. Behind their backs, Congress gave the Independent Payment Advisory Board (IPAB) the authority to slash Medicare costs so badly that Congress wanted plausible deniability – in other words, someone else to blame. Not only can Congress do little about the IPAB, but much of the control over what the IPAB cuts out of the Medicare budget is outside the hands of voters as well. The IPAB has almost zero accountability and is purposely set up to operate much like the Federal Reserve Board is set up. This is the perfect mechanism to phase-out Medicare.

According to Nicolas Tate, author of "ObamaCare Survival Guide":

> The biggest spending cuts [for seniors] will come in two areas: reduced number of plans available and reduced benefits in the Medicare Advantage program (which allows enrollees to use private insurance to supplement their basic Medicare coverage), and reduced payment rates to doctors who care for Medicare patients.[219]

ObamaCare increases prescription and preventative care coverage for seniors. It also puts a cap on how much insurers can charge seniors based on their age.[220] ObamaCare fills in a gap for enrollees who purchase prescription drugs through the Medicare Part D program. (That coverage gap is often referred to as the doughnut hole.) Currently, people who are eligible for Medicare but who have not signed up would count as "old" eligibles so the federal government will continue paying 57% of the cost to the states. The federal government will pay 97% for "newly" eligible Medicare enrollees until 2020.[221] After 2020, it is unclear if the federal government will pay 57% or transfer the entire cost of Medicare from the "newly" eligible Medicare applicants to the states. The current push to get everyone into the ObamaCare system has strained state budgets since many of the people applying are not the 97% federal coverage "newly" eligible. Consequently, this creates a cost for the states that they didn't have previously.

The few goodies Congress gave seniors are a distraction from the fact that seniors will fund over half of the cost of the $1 trillion ObamaCare bill. Rather than extend Medicare's solvency by reapplying the savings into the Medicare program, $716 billion cuts to the future Medicare budget will fund the new ObamaCare programs. Seniors can expect at least $1355 less per dollar per year on their medical care.[222] Ironically, this cut will affect 5,000 home health care companies and 500,000 care provider jobs.[223] This means the cuts for senior care will affect many more people than just seniors.

The progressives made light of the $716 billion cut to Medicare saying that it was only about costs and not about benefits.[224] Part of this argument is based on cutting future costs, while also asserting that Medicare funding remains the same. If you increase the Medicare population by 30%, by adding the new baby boomers to the current system,[225] there will be many more people who will need services. If the Medicare budget stays the same, then there is less money to go around per patient, so it is effectively cutting benefits along with costs. Then add the cost of inflation to the Medicare and the fixed budget doesn't go as far as it did prior to the passage of the ACA. Of necessity, benefits will need to be rationed because there is only so much funding to go around. Logically, have you ever seen any program that cut deeply into current and future costs that did not affect the programs benefits?

Publicists for ObamaCare insist that these cuts would expand and improve care for seniors while saying it "isn't really a cut, its health care reform."[226] By reform, they mean that the payments will be so low that many plans and care providers will not participate in the system. If, as the government insists, there is three-fourths of a trillion dollars of fraud and waste built into the Medicare system as it currently stands and the government is only addressing the issue after 40 years, then that is proof that the government is not capable of running an even larger program called ObamaCare.

With the 30% reduction in Medicare payments to doctors and hospitals over the next three years, by 2019, the payment rates will be lower than under Medicaid.[227] When payment becomes that low, most seniors will not be able to keep their doctors. According to Lawrence Hunter and Peter Ferrara, posted in the Wall Street Journal, the cuts are much worse that $716 billion out of Medicare because that amount does not include any cuts that will happen from the IPAB:

> Altogether, ObamaCare cuts $818 billion from Medicare Part A (hospital insurance) from 2014-2023, the first 10 years of its full implementation, and $3.2 trillion over the first 20 years, 2014-2033. Adding in ObamaCare cuts for Medicare Part B (physician's fees and other services) brings the total cut to $1.05 trillion over the first 10 years and $4.95 trillion over the first 20 years.[228]

Obamacare raids Medicare to pay for other new programs

Projected Medicare savings from Obamacare don't improve the program. Instead, they pay for other new programs created under the law that aren't even for seniors. By slashing reimbursement rates instead of introducing real reform, the health law jeopardizes seniors' access to providers.

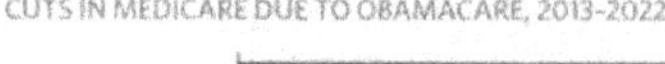

CUTS IN MEDICARE DUE TO OBAMACARE, 2013-2022

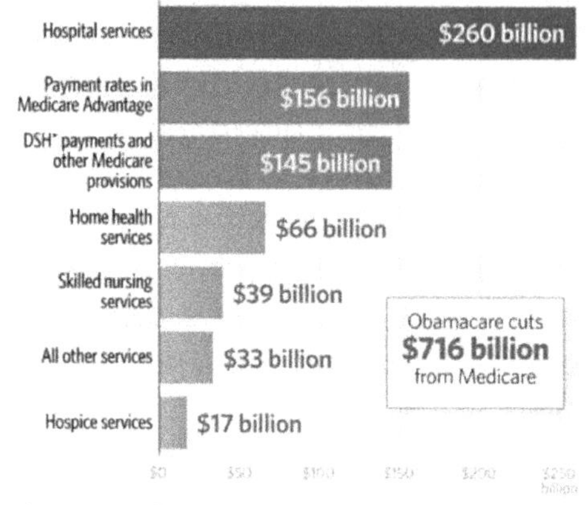

Source: Congressional Budget Office report.

* Disproportionate Share Hospital, meaning payments that go to hospitals that serve a large number of low-income patients.

Chart 10 • Medicare at Risk heritage.org

Those seniors with higher incomes will be paying more for Medicare D premiums.[229] Significant revenue raised from the new Medicare hospital taxes will not go back into the Medicare system.[230] A reporter did an investigation in North Carolina posing as a Medicare beneficiary looking for a doctor. Out of 200 doctors, about half said they no longer accepted new Medicare patients.[231] This will only get worse in the future as more money is shifted away from Medicare. Because of the enormous Medicaid expansion in enrollees, this will directly affect seniors in the quality and timeliness of their doctor visits since the expansion did not come with additional medical staff to absorb the vast increase in patient load. Instead, there are heavy cuts to doctors, hospitals and insurers that will make the problem worse by making it harder to get quality, timely services. There will be rationed care.

Avik Roy, Forbes Staff, summed up the semantics over seniors funding a large portion of other ObamaCare entitlements with severe Medicare cuts stated:

> There's an intellectually honest case to make in support of ObamaCare's Medicare cuts. If you believe that taking money out of Medicare in order to expand subsidies of coverage for younger Americans is a

> good thing, then you have every reason to support what ObamaCare did to Medicare. But it's not intellectually honest to claim that these [$768 billion] cuts are inconsequential, or that they're offset by relatively trivial spending [$52 billion] on "new benefits." As President Obama recently put it, "You can't just make stuff up."[232]

Hospitals policies are going to get ugly for elderly patients because ObamaCare has tied their hands. One example of how lower reimbursement affects hospital care is that for every $1,000 that a hospital loses in Medicare reimbursement, there is a 6 to 8 percent increase of dying from a heart attack.[233] Also, consider that hospitals spending the least on elderly patients are actually given bonuses, while those who spend more on the elderly will face demerits.[234] Beginning on October 1, 2012, Section 3001 states that hospitals are fined for readmitting a patient for the same medical problem within 30 days after discharge. This will have unintended consequences for the elderly who relapse frequently with heart or lung diseases. According to Dr. Elaina F. George, "they will be treated as outpatients for as long as possible to avoid fines."[235] Furthermore, "There will be a push to avoid inpatient admissions on the one hand while discharging patients as quickly as possible on the other. Patients may be allowed to become sicker before they are admitted, making overall outcomes more tenuous."[236]

Home health care services saved the Medicare program $2.8 billion dollars over a three-year period. Much of the savings legitimately comes from fewer hospital readmissions and having less chance of contracting other infections.[237] Yet, according to Dan Weber, President of the Association of Mature American Citizens, on January 1, 2014, $22 billion dollars, was cut from the home health care services for seniors ages 60 and above.[238] This cut will affect 3.5 million poor and ill homebound seniors. Typically, these people are older, poorer and sicker than the general Medicare population and many are in rural areas where they can't travel to a city for care.

Section 4103 provides for wellness plan monitoring. While it is nice to have options for wellness plans for Medicare, there are some concerns in section (F) page 437. The Secretary will be exploring technology that integrates with electronic medical records. This will aid in "management of and adherence to provider recommendations in order to improve the health status of beneficiaries." This provision reminds me of a medical parole officer when the government will be involved with management of and adherence to a wellness plan for obesity or other conditions they deem as chronic.

One of the lower blows the administration has done was to publicize Medicare Physician payment data out of context. I'll explain more about this in the doctor section below.

Another low blow was AARP's support of this bill. They did not represent the best interests of seniors. Everyone who is as angry as I was about this should switch to the alternative Association of Mature American Citizens, AMAC.

While there is a full-scale media attack on doctors, the government wastes $1.2 billion dollars on Serco to employ 10,000 people to support Medicare and Medicaid.[239] What do they do? Almost nothing because the exchange enrollments have stopped and there are few who are actually taking applications. The rest of the employees sit for weeks at a time. Serco has been banned from the United Kingdom for overbilling the government for monitoring dead or imprisoned people. They were also fined $15 million in Australia for shady monitoring of their asylum detention centers.[240] If the government was really interested in controlling fraud, they would start by hiring reputable companies and have standards for exchange navigators.

As Ed Morrissey put it, one of the problems with the current system is that we have "third parties involved in too many health-care provider transactions. ObamaCare makes that worse, and creates a strong disincentive for providers to boot."[241] "Time to throw it out and start over, and focus on removing third parties from all transactions but hospitalization and catastrophic care."[242]

Medicare Advantage

Another program that tremendously helps seniors is Medicare Advantage, which covers about 30% of those enrolled in Medicare. This is the private insurance plan launched in 2003 that supplements Medicare benefits because Medicare usually only covers 60% of the medical costs. The government website states that ObamaCare doesn't cut benefits, yet they say they reduce payments to Medicare Advantage because it "is run by private insurers and costs $1,000 more per person."[243] Moreover, they claim that Medicare Advantage is causing a tax burden that is disproportionate to the amount of people it helps.[244] Obviously, they haven't considered exponentially larger tax burden of ObamaCare. The other issue is that they really haven't cut costs, but have just shifted it to the privately insured people.[245]

Health Care Law Cuts to Medicare Advantage Services in 2017

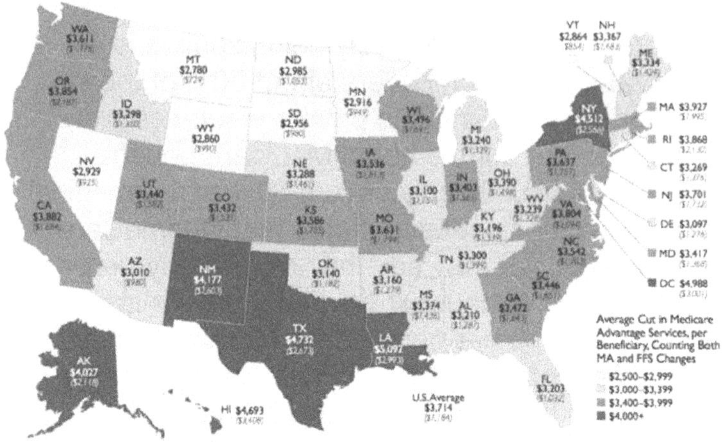

There appears to be many discrepancies in information about the Medicare Advantage budget. One report was from the Obama administration that the payment would reduce slightly.[246] Several insurance analysts quantified that a slight reduction would be as much as 3.5%.[247] It appears the analysts were right because in a town hall meeting with Congressman Bill Cassidy in March 2014, Congress did vote a $300 billion (3.5%) cut out of Medicare Advantage. This cut is over and above the scheduled 6% cut that was to happen in 2014. I don't know how the reimbursement rates, scheduled to increase by 4%, in 2015 fits into this calculation.[248] So far, funding cuts have not been widely publicized because seniors would notice. Their premiums would increase and their benefits would be reduced $35 to $75 per month.[249] "According to the Congressional Budget Office these senior citizens will get about $68 less a month in Medicare Advantage benefits because of ObamaCare."[250] It is expected that more cuts to this program will not be revisited until after the 2014 vote.

Although it is currently hard to tell how much Medicare Advantage will be phased out by ObamaCare, the chart above is a chart showing the cuts to Medicare Advantage in 2017. ObamaCare reduces Medicare Advantage funding by

27%, meaning that by 2017, there will be $3,700 less per year for each senior.[251]

Avik Roy, reported in Forbes, his conclusion that "Medicare Advantage offers seniors higher-quality care at a lower cost than government-run Medicare. ObamaCare should have sought to save money by expanding the program, instead of undermining it."[252]

Independent Payment Advisory Board (IPAB)

Section 3403, creates the Independent Payment Advisory Board (IPAB) that has total control over the Medicare budget going to 15 unelected members who are appointed by the President and confirmed by the Senate. Congress purposely and unconstitutionally,[253] delegated total power to the IPAB. The law unconstitutionally insulates the IPAB from judicial review.[254] It also keeps the board largely outside of Congressional control and out of the control of voters. This board can operate with virtually no accountability, much like the Federal Reserve Board.

Although the IPAB is supposed to be overseen by advisory reports to the President and the Senate, there is no authority to make any changes absent a 3/5 super-majority vote in Congress. Obama himself has called for a "substantial expansion of IPAB's already unprecedented powers."[255] This means that there are already plans to expand IPAB authority from controlling only Medicare costs to all of the other ObamaCare programs, which includes Medicaid.

Earlier, I had mentioned that Obama had talked about creating a single-payer system. Creation of the IPAB is the single most effect provision in ObamaCare in making socialized medicine into a single-payer system where the government monopolizes the purse strings.[256]

Medicaid

The total Medicaid budget is around $431 billion dollars with 58% ($251 billion) prior to adding new enrollees.[257] States pay about 22 to 30 percent of their budgets on Medicaid.[258]

According to Heritage.org, "On average, physicians in Medicare are paid 81 percent of private payment; physicians in Medicaid are paid 56 percent of private payment." In 2008, "Florida's Medicaid reimbursements averaged 63 percent of Medicare fees for all services, and 55 percent of Medicare fees for primary care."[259] Medicaid has now been moved from serving as a temporary safety net, to a permanent alternative to private insurance.[260] Medicaid appears to be the default option for ObamaCare, and is designed to move to a one-size-fits-all socialized program that eventually absorbs all other medical programs.

According to Betsy McCaughey, citing a University of Virginia study, "Medicaid patients were twice as likely to die in the hospital after surgery as patients with private coverage."[261] Medicaid patients were 13% more likely to die than patients with no insurance at all.[262] Her conclusion is, "What the research shows is that Medicaid patients get worse care but not cheaper care."[263] Not only do many people with Medicaid suffer from the lack of proper care, but there is a lot of cost-shifting onto people with private insurance. So far, the cost-shifting is about $1500 per family, but as Medicaid rolls increase, the premium will go higher.[264] McCaughey notes, "The more Medicaid is expanded, the higher private premiums will go. As a taxpayer, you pay for Medicaid twice – first when you pay your federal taxes, and again when you pay your own insurance bill."[265]

The way that Medicare is being downsized, I would expect the elderly to eventually be funneled into the Medicaid program. Moving millions of people into an already swollen system and then lowering the payments, does not incentivize health care providers to take these patients. Consequently, paying for Medicaid health insurance does not guarantee that one can get benefits. Of necessity, there will be less quality of care, longer wait times, and rationed benefits.

According to Opinion Research Corporation in their 2010 survey, "67 percent of new Medicaid enrollees would not be able to find a suitable primary care physician in their area."[266] The federal government pays an average of 57% of the cost of Medicaid to the state.[267] Primary care physicians will receive the Medicare rate for Medicaid patients for 2013 and 2014.[268] The problem will come in 2015 when the federal government dumps an unfunded mandate onto the states. When the federal government stops paying, either the states will have to increase their Medicaid funding, or they will need to cut back on Medicaid physician payments, or some combination of both.

There are many unintended consequences of such sweeping legislation written mostly by academics and people who have an agenda. Traditionally, Medicaid has provided health care coverage for low-income parents, children, and disabled individuals. According to Bobby Jindal, Governor of Louisiana, "The law provides a richer federal match for states' coverage of childless adults than Medicaid programs receive for covering individuals with disabilities. That's a case of skewed priorities if I ever heard of one."[269] He further noted that there is already a waiting list of over half-a-million disabled people. Adding more people to the Medicaid rolls will make it even harder for disabled people to get the care they need.

According to Michael D. Tanner of the Cato Institute, citing a study in the New England Journal of Medicine, "Individuals posing as mothers of children with serious medical conditions were denied an appointment 66% of the time if they said that their child was on Medicaid (or the related CHIP), compared with 11% for private insurance, a ratio of 6 to 1."[270] Moreover, he cites studies regarding appointment wait times,

> "Even when doctors do still treat Medicaid patients, they often have a harder time getting appointments and face longer wait times. One study found that among clinics that accepted both privately insured children and those enrolled in Medicaid, the average wait time for an appointment was 42 days for Medicaid compared to just 20 days for the privately insured."[271]

Unintended consequences of longer wait times if a newly insured Medicaid patient can find a doctor is that sometimes they can't wait to see a the doctor. That means that emergency rooms become overburdened with patients and the real emergencies have longer wait times imposed on them. Emergency rooms charge much more for treatment than a doctor visit.[272]

If you are 55 to 64, there is an archaic law that a state can seize your estate to pay for any Medicaid costs paid out for your health care.[273] Washington State has dug up the 25-year-old law and is now enforcing it to recoup Medicaid costs paid out by the State. Likewise, other states are interested in following Washington's lead. Not only are people forced to participate in ObamaCare, but also they have to pay more to the government after they die. Effectively, this means that people who obtain Medicaid health insurance will not only pay for insurance on a monthly basis or by penalties but their Medicaid treatments will be like getting a government loan for health care services. If the Medicare seniors are eventually funneled into Medicaid, they have a lot more to lose than the Medicare losses listed in the section above.

Not to be outdone by Medicare or by businesses, Medicaid also has a Wellness program centered on prevention or management of chronic diseases.[274] Chronic disease in this section is considered as smoking, obesity, lowering cholesterol and blood pressure, and diabetes.[275] A sample of the programs is 1) controlling food at school and in a "safe environment", 2) physical exercise at school, 3) assessing and implementing worksite wellness "programming and incentives," 4) reducing racial and ethnic disparities, and 5) addressing "special populations' needs."[276] At first, there is a lot of grant money, awarded at the discretion of the Secretary, to institute those programs, but the bigger issue is when do these programs become compulsory? Again, the reports are extensive and there are many privacy issues regarding who gets what information and how they get it.

Health Insurance

My first questions of Obamacare is "What's in it for the health insurance and the drug companies? What would make them agree to all the regulations, reports, major revisions in how they do business and a list of items that must be covered? One part of the answer is that the government gave them a monopoly on 30 million[277] new, mandatory sign-up customers via imposition of the individual mandate. The government also promised to pay them guaranteed money for some of these people too. Not only do they get more customers to spread the risk around, but compliant health insurances have a tying arrangement with the government.

According to Allen West, quoting Brian Mast, spokesperson for eHealthInsurance:

> "Health insurance premiums are increasing primarily because of the new required provisions for 2014 Affordable Care Act compliant plans, including guaranteed issue, essential health benefits, modified community rating and minimum actuarial values. It is also likely that health insurance companies expected additional risk in the risk pool, because people with pre-existing conditions could no longer be denied coverage, and may have priced their plans higher to accommodate for this risk."[278]

Premiums have skyrocketed for everyone, in some states it went up 80-90%.[279] After the November 2014 elections and even after the open enrollment starts on November 15, many insurances have plans to raise their premiums 100%.[280] This summer will be a continual media blitz about premium hikes and political damage control. Smokers pay up to 50% more for their premiums as a "smoking surcharge."[281] As if the monthly premiums are not bad enough, there are high deductibles of multi-thousands of dollars, and out-of-pocket costs for tests and services not covered by the insurance or Obamacare.

Health insurances can pass on government taxes to the consumers, which will add $300-400 per year to premiums of a family of 4[282] or $277 per year for an individual.[283] The insurances can also pass on losses to consumers by raising premiums with little accountability. There are two provisions to control how much insurances can raise premiums. One is the government's willingness to throw an offending health insurance provider off the preferred health insurance compliance list. The other is that insurances must maintain a medical loss ratio. That means that insurances must spend a certain percentage of their income on benefits or they will be non-compliant with the medical loss ratio. However, considering the industry losses from not having enough of the healthy people sign up, the losses are substantial enough that insurances that comply with the medical loss ratio won't keep premiums down at this point.

Robert Laszewski, a prominent health insurance consultant, quoted by Jeffrey H. Anderson, illuminates why the insurance bailout serves a dual function that promotes government control over private health insurance while advancing a single-payer agenda:

> "ObamaCare contains a 'Reinsurance Program that caps big claim costs for insurers (individual plans only).' He writes that 'in 2014, 80% of individual costs between $45,000 and $250,000 are paid by the government [read: *by taxpayers*], for example.
>
> In other words, insurance purchased through ObamaCare's government-run exchanges isn't even full-fledged private insurance; rather, it's a sort of private-public hybrid. Private insurance companies pay for costs below $45,000, then taxpayers generously pick up the tab—a tab that their president hasn't ever bothered to tell them he has opened up on their behalf—for four-fifths of the next $200,000-plus worth of costs. In this way, and so many others, ObamaCare takes a major step toward the government monopoly over American medicine ('single payer') that liberals drool about in their sleep."[284]

Additionally, there is a Risk Corridor program that helps insurances so that they are not responsible to pay for all of the costs, nor do they have to absorb all the losses. "Once an insurance company covers that initial 2 percent in unexpected costs, taxpayers will cover at least 80 percent of any additional costs the insurer accrues."[285]

In other words, public or private health insurances will not be absorbing the losses because they can raise premiums and there are programs that pass on certain costs. These mechanisms are an unofficial bailout of insurance companies. In the end, ObamaCare is like double taxation on corporations. The taxpayers are mandated to pay once by the individual mandate legislation, and then they pay twice because they pay through their tax dollars. But third-payer health insurances won't last forever. The way ObamaCare is set up; eventually health care insurances will be outdated and replaced by a single-payer system.

Obtaining and keeping health insurance is never an easy task. As of April 1, open enrollment for ObamaCare was closed until November 2014, unless a person experiences a qualifying life event such as marriage, loss of a job, etc. "The law, which requires nearly all Americans to be insured or pay a fine, bans insurers from rejecting customers because of poor health. The companies say that makes it too risky to sell to individuals year-round."[286] This means that insurances wanted to mitigate their losses. They did not want sick or high-risk people without a high percentage of healthy enrollees. Otherwise, they would not be able to make a profit.

At present, health insurances and drug companies seem to have an intermediary function of being the scapegoat during the transition while the government stays quiet about who is really causing the premiums to go up. The government ties the health insurance businesses up through presidential and congressional mandates designed to fail. How can a business set a premium when they must take everyone without a cap on benefits and yet they cannot ask about a person's health status? As a business, this is a recipe for financial disaster. When insurances continue raising premiums, it will ensure that the voters scream out enough that health care is a one-issue platform and hurts democratic votes. At that point, then the single payer system will be the government "fix" that cuts out health insurance entirely.

According to Ezekiel Emanuel, one of the architects of ObamaCare in New Republic:

> "The accountable care organizations (ACOs) and hospital systems will begin competing directly in the exchanges and for exclusive contracts with employers. These new organizations are delivery systems with networks of physicians and hospitals that provide comprehensive care. This health delivery structure is in its infancy. Today there are hundreds of these organizations being created and gaining experience within government sponsored programs or getting contracts from private insurers. They are developing and testing ways to coordinate, standardize, and provide care more efficiently and at consistent higher quality standards. Over the next decade, many of these ACOs and hospital systems will succeed at integrating all the components of care and provide efficient, coordinated care. They will have the physician and hospital networks. They will have standardized, guideline driven care plans for most major conditions and procedures to increase efficiency. They will have figured out how to harness their electronic medical records to better identify patients who will become sick and how to intervene early as well as how to care for the well-identified chronically ill so as to reduce costs."[287]

Even as the government conspires to take over health care, the free market is poised to fill the huge health care void created by Obamacare. I discuss ACOs more thoroughly in the solutions section below.

One of the reasons that insurance premiums have gone up is the mandatory items for coverage that insurances shall provide in order to be compliant with ObamaCare. Sally Pipes, quoting the Council for Affordable Health Insurance found that, "Mandated benefits increase the cost of basic health coverage by as much as 50%.[288] You can find a list of all mandatory benefits at https://www.healthcare.gov/what-does-marketplace-health-insurance-cover/. Some of the more interesting sections are the preventative services that are broken into three sections - adults, women and children at: https://www.health care.gov/what-are-my-preventive-care-benefits/.

Another reason for the high prices is geography and the lack of market competition. The Red states, which have large rural areas, had their premiums raise an average of 78%, while Blue states had their premiums raise an average of 50%.[289] Rural areas are hit hard with high, unaffordable premiums. For instance, the New York Times reports:

> "Of the roughly 2,500 counties served by the federal exchange, more than half, or 58 percent, have plans offered by just one or two insurance carriers, according to an analysis by The Times of county-level data provided by the Department of Health and Human Services. In about 530 counties, only a single insurer is participating. The analysis suggests that the ambitions of the Affordable Care Act to increase competition have unfolded unevenly, at least in the early going, and have not addressed many of the factors that contribute to high prices."[290]

I rearranged the data from a survey article by Richard Pollock printed in the Washington Examiner.[291] The article surveyed 16 cities in different parts of the U.S. about health insurances, doctors, and hospitals. The percentage of health insurances participating in the exchanges ranged from 17-80% with the lowest percentage in Naples/Ft. Myers, Florida and the highest number of insurances in the exchange in Roanoke, Virginia. What is more telling than the numbers are the two reasons people choose health insurance – access and price. Access has been severely limited because many insurances, hospitals, and especially doctors choose not to join the exchanges. In Seattle, Children's Hospital was blocked from the exchange. In other places, the nearest participating hospital was over an hour away. Rural areas have issues finding a competitive health insurance since there is only one available, so the premiums go up 30-50%. Atlanta's premium went up 80-100% from what it was last year. Very few exchanges allowed specialized cancer treatment hospitals to participate.

Limiting insurance costs under ObamaCare means rationing the quality and quantity of care. Not only are the insurances limiting their exposure for higher costs by not accepting any more applications, but they also limit what they will pay. For instance, most insurances in the exchange either exclude top cancer hospitals or severely limit what they will pay for cancer treatment.[292]

Insurances have many issues that ObamaCare has made much worse by removing the competitive free market. When government sets the prices and limits who can be in the exchange, what services are covered, who is paid, and how much people must pay, there is no free market and therefore the costs skyrocket. I've never been a fan of market pooling because it has only helped groups of people rather than the individuals. Although the entire health care model as it was before ObamaCare had severe flaws, it still could be fixed with proper incentives rather than mandates and penalties. Decent health care is a right – that's another matter discussed in the solutions section below.

Business

The ACA is fairly complex regarding businesses, workers, citizens, the medical industry and insurances, but all of the legislation leads to the same place – funneling everyone into the ObamaCare system. Even though there are private health care insurances tightly controlled by the government, it will be very hard for health insurances outside of the exchanges or those insurances not in compliance with government mandates to survive.

Technically, HR 3590 does not mandate an employer to offer government approved health care to employees. However, if the business has at least 50 full-time employees (working 30 or more hours) and if one of those employees obtains a health care premium credit through an exchange, the employer shall pay a fine of $2,000 per employee.[293]

Earlier, I mentioned that the ACA states and the legislative history supports that Congress meant to give the subsidies through state exchanges as a way to encourage states to participate in ObamaCare. The IRS acted outside of its authority by reforming the law to read ALL exchanges, so that would mean federal and state exchanges. Oklahoma has a pending legal challenge in Federal Court that 1) the IRS acted outside of its scope of authority and 2) large businesses in states that do not have a state exchange do not need to comply with ObamaCare because there are no employees who can go through a state exchange to trigger the employer penalty clause. Remember that non-participating states actually do better economically because they are not saddled with such high insurance premiums and employee reporting costs. Participating states are at a disadvantage because their labor costs are much higher than non-participating states due to ObamaCare taxes.

There are some temporary credits for small businesses to transition with health insurance, but these end in 2015. As part of the exchanges, small employers with less than 50 employees can obtain insurance through the exchange in a program called Small Business Health Options Program (SHOP). There are tax credits available for employers with less than 25-full-time employees.[294]

For those businesses with over 100 employees, employers can opt to participate in an employee wellness program. The law allows these employers to pay for up to 50% of the health care premium. On the other hand, almost half of 600 large employers surveyed will make participation in the employee wellness programs mandatory or the employee will face substantial fines for non-participation.[295] For large businesses that run their own health insurance in-house, the legislation will not affect them much, if at all.

The rest of the business section is written for those businesses that fall within the scope of the employer mandate. Since 48% of the population receives health insurance through their employers, Congress tried to conscript business to pay into Obamacare and force employees into compliance.

As part of the "non-discrimination" language in ObamaCare, employers cannot provide more generous health insurance benefits or higher employer contributions to highly-compensated employees. Although enforcement has been suspended for now by the IRS.

Prior to HR. 3950 being passed, employers paid an average of 70-80% of the cost of employee premiums.[296] According to Nicholas Tate, "On average, employers pay about $13,500 per employee for health insurance, and that employees only pay about 30 percent — $4,000, on average — of the total amount in any given year. That's $333 a month per employee."[297] Now, the employers must offer insurance to all employees equally and cannot ask the worker to pay more than 9.5% of the household income. The business is required to certify **household** income for the IRS. The issues that come from employers knowing household income and reporting it for and to the IRS really crosses the privacy line for citizens and the implications are far wider than just ObamaCare eligibility. Remember that 159 agencies and boards working with ObamaCare will also have this information.

There are many other perversions that come out of these perverted health care laws. What happens to businesses and their employees has crushing consequences to families and lower income individuals.

Another aspect of the business/employee health care issue has to do with mixing employee health care and family eligibility for the exchange. If one family member has health care provided by their employer, then the other family members will not be eligible for a subsidy. This may affect 13 million lower-income families because they cannot afford the ObamaCare insurance without the subsidies.[298] Right off the ObamaCare website, the administration owns up to the "unforeseen effects" and recommends that employers stop "offering unaffordable coverage for spouses who will then become eligible for cost assistance through the Health Insurance."[299] Another unintended family consequence is that couples might decide not get married because this penalizes family members.

We discussed the skyrocketing insurance premiums in the last section. Available business options depend on how many people are employed by the company on a full-time basis. The federal definition of full-time is 30 or more hours per week. If a business has 50 to 99 employees, they must either pay health insurance premiums for full-time employees, or pay a fine of $2,000 per employee to the government. For many businesses, the $2,000 penalty is much cheaper than "affordable" health insurance.

At present, the exchanges serve individuals and small businesses. In businesses that have at least 50 full-time people, the employee must sign up for health care through their employer unless the employer does not provide adequate coverage or the employer does provide coverage but the cost to the employee exceeds 9.5% of the household income. When employees earn less than 400% of the federal poverty level and the cost of insurance is between 8 to 9.8% of the family household income, employers must offer them free choice vouchers.[300] A free choice voucher allows the employee to use the employer's insurance money towards purchasing a plan off the exchange. The voucher also allows the employee to take advantage of the subsidies so the cost should be less for the employee than if he or she were covered for insurance through the employer. Insurance obtained through the employer is not eligible for subsidies.

Another perversion is what happens to the workforce. To avoid the significant, additional costs incurred from having to supply everyone with health insurance, businesses have been cutting hours from 40 hours per week to under 30 hours per week. Many businesses have also stopped hiring. Where businesses would expand and spend money on additional employees, the extra costs associated with ObamaCare has put heavy burdens on many businesses so they can't afford to hire more people. Instead, more businesses will turn to independent contractors, export their jobs overseas, or depend more on automated services. Many small and medium businesses will be forced to close.

Consider that for tax purposes, volunteers are considered as employees. This means that organizations offering necessary services such as a volunteer firefighting force are technically harboring employees, so they must offer health insurance to the volunteers. It is estimated from over 1 million fire stations that 87% of the firefighters are volunteers.[301] This requirement will shut the volunteers down if there are 50 or more volunteers in the organization.

ObamaCare directly harms the lower-income workers in several ways. The burden falls disproportionately heavily on "non-whites, high-school drop-outs, and women."[302] As Sally Pipes says, "As a percentage of salary, the per-worker cost of providing health insurance is much higher for low-income workers than it is for high-income workers."[303] Most businesses provide health care to higher end workers as a way to incentivize top talent to stay with the business. Lower-income workers are expendable and easily replaced in the eyes of business. According to Sally Pipes, "74 percent of firms surveyed plan to pass the law's higher costs on to their employees by changing plan options, restricting eligibility, or increasing deductibles or co-pays."[304]

The Congressional Budget Office (CBO) already knows how much of a strain will be put on businesses and estimates close to $52 billion in tax penalties will be collected from businesses between 2014 and 2019. The CBO is literally counting on the penalties to provide ObamaCare funding. According to John Rossomando, quoting the CBO, "Approximately 650,000 mainly lower-paid and lower-skilled workers could find themselves out of a job as a result of the health care law's implementation during the second half of the decade."[305]

According to Guy Benson, citing a report from the Congressional Budget Office,

> "The Affordable Care Act will also reduce the number of fulltime workers by more than 2 million in coming years, congressional budget analysts said in the most detailed analysis of the law's impact on jobs. The CBO said the law's impact on jobs would be mostly

> felt starting after 2016. The agency previously estimated that the economy would have 800,000 fewer jobs as a result of the law. The impact is likely to be most felt, the CBO said, among low-wage workers. The agency said that most of the effect would come from Americans deciding not to seek work as a result of the ACA's impact on the economy. Some workers may forgo employment, while others may reduce hours, for an equivalent of at least 2 million fulltime workers dropping out of the labor force."[306]

It helps to understand that employee costs are not just the minimum wage per hour that the person is hired at. For instance, if an employee receives $7.25 per hour, employers also pay payroll taxes, unemployment taxes, and disability insurance premiums. Now add on mandatory health insurance. That cost will add another $1.79 per hour cost to a single employee or $5.51 per hour for an employee with dependents.[307] In Betsy McCaughey's words, "Hiring a minimum wage worker will be costly, but hiring a minimum wage worker with a family will be prohibitive."[308] When a business is up against that kind of cost, they don't have a lot of choice. They can either pay the federal fines, replace full-time employees with part-time workers, or they can automate services.[309]

Consider that the $2,000 penalty per full-time worker attaches to whether the employee obtains a subsidy from the exchange. An employer is safer if they hire a person from a wealthy family rather than a poor family. That way the employee would be less likely to trigger the employer penalty because the household income would make them less likely to qualify for a subsidy through the exchange. This is another perversion that results in the lower-income workers being discriminated against in order to avoid business penalties.

When people are having their employment hours cut and they can't find a job, many people are suffering from this legislation. As Obama reminds us, these people just need to prioritize health care and do without phones and cable.

These words of wisdom come on the heels of the low income families who are struggling to survive, but never mind - they will have their health care if nothing else. Moreover, the IRS will prosecute businesses employing between 50-99 people if they dump employees into the exchange without certifying under penalty of perjury that ObamaCare was a motivating factor in their staffing decisions. In Gary DeMar's words, "To avoid ObamaCare costs you must swear that you are not trying to avoid Obamacare costs."[310]

Grandfather Status

> *"If you like your doctor, you will be able to keep your doctor. Period. If you like your health care plan, you will be able to keep your health care plan. Period. No one will take it away. No matter what." Barack Obama*

Prior to ObamaCare passing in 2010, a 2009 Gallup poll stated that the "majority of Americans were satisfied with their medical plans. The majority of uninsured were satisfied with their medical care and costs."[311] There was even a 79% satisfaction rating with Medicare and Medicaid patients.[312]

If you like your health care, can you really keep it?

President Obama promised reform would not affect existing coverage. While it remains uncertain exactly how many Americans will lose employer-sponsored plans under Obamacare, studies show it will be millions.

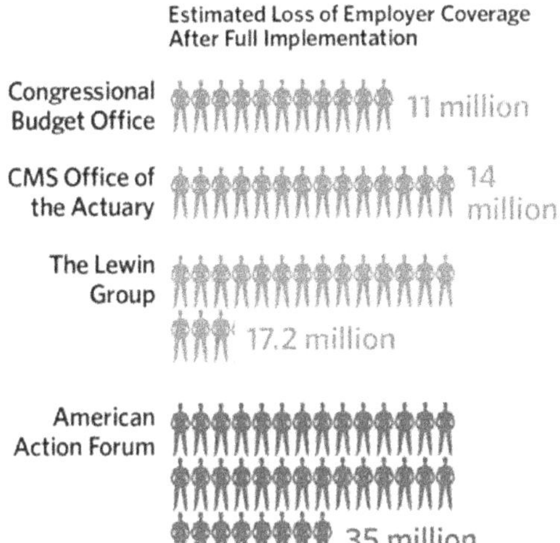

Sources: Congressional Budget Office, March 2010; CMS Office of the Actuary, April 2010; The Lewin Group, June 2010; and the American Action Forum, May 2010.

Obamacare in Pictures heritage.org

If you like your insurance plan, doctor, or whatever, you can keep it - anything to minimize the threat of administrative failure and get public buy-in for the legislation. That is the basis for the grandfather status. For those people who have health insurance, ObamaCare should not affect them . . . unless their plan is non-compliant. If the plan meets certain criteria, then it enters into a grandfather status allowing individuals to keep their plan and by extension, their doctor. If it does not meet the criteria, then they lose their health care and must find new, compliant private health care or sign up for ObamaCare.

According to the government Health Care Reform Survey 2011-2012, by the end of 2013, 49% of the plans would retain their grandfather status.[313] In actuality, it was less than 30% of employers' plans that retained their grandfather status as of March 2012.[314] The Justice Department reported that according to DHHS, the majority of the plans will lose their grandfather status by the end of 2013, so the incremental "transition" does not significantly undermine the governments interests.[315] When the government uses the word "transition" it assumes that everyone will be eventually funneled into ObamaCare, the only issue is how long this will take.

HSAs – Health Flexible Spending Arrangements

Health Savings Accounts were started by the Bush administration to help healthy people to afford occasional medical expenses. According to George W. Bush, "This meant that they would pay their own health expenses, and would be able to keep any money left over."[316] Also, "they had incentives to stay healthy, shop for good deals, and negotiate better prices."[317] According to America's Health Insurance Plans, 10 million Americans possessed these plans.[318] Since ObamaCare relies on young invincibles, HSAs will be phased out and these people funneled into exchanges. The transition started by limiting what the HSA could be used for by stating that these funds cannot purchase over-the-counter items and that any non-medically eligible withdrawal will incur higher penalties.

Prescriptions

The current FDA regulations take years of testing and a lot of money to bring to the market. It costs the pharmaceuticals an average of 1.3 billion to bring a new drug to the market.[319] While this can be to minimize lawsuits, it stymies innovation and incentive to bring life-saving medicine to patients. Add socialized medicine to the equation, and the only market for new drugs will be outside of the United States; thus hobbling the greatest life-saving research and development group on the planet.

On the other hand, pharmaceutical companies sold us out by being greedy, like the insurance companies, and likewise benefits from the additional customers.

An early analysis of medications received by ObamaCare enrollees shows they are more likely to use expensive specialty drugs than private insurance. Other differences according to Sarah Jean Seman:

> ObamaCare users received 35 percent more pain medication, 27 percent more medication to control seizures, and 14 percent more antidepressants than the privately insured. The proportion of contraceptives

actually dropped 31 percent among ObamaCare enrollees.[320]

I'm sure that a lot of the differences reflect a sicker pool of people who were among the first enrollees. A formulary is a list of drugs that the insurance will pay for. Private insurances tend to have drug formularies with cheap drugs and benefit caps to control their costs. If the drug is not on the list then the patient must pay out-of-pocket for the drug and typically that cost does not count toward a deductible or towards a maximum out of pocket amount paid. This is particularly difficult towards cancer treatments, lupus or multiple sclerosis where one medication can cost $62,000.[321] Since these medications are not already part of the mandated benefits, if Obamacare does decide to add them to the formularies, then premiums go up or networks and providers are further reduced. Otherwise, people either pay for medications or go without them.

Obamacare did not make treatment available to these people. It made the problem worse and the issue still needs to be solved.

Hospitals

Hospital funding was severely cut by Obamacare. While several states had medical loss ratios (MLRs), Obamacare mandates hospitals in participating states to have them. A medical loss ratio keeps hospital profits low by mandating how much money goes towards running the hospital vs. administrative overhead. In the 15 states that had MLRs, the mandates resulted in "higher premiums, less competition, and fewer choices."[322]

The cuts are severe enough that 15% more hospitals will operate in the red.[323] Others will close or "be forced to operate in an environment of scarcity, with fewer nurses on the floor, fewer cleaners, longer waits for high-tech diagnostic tests. That will affect all patients."[324] This will especially affect smaller hospitals, rural hospitals, and those with emergency rooms.

One big issue is in how hospitals will be evaluated. Evaluations are not patient-centered, but rather are performance based. ObamaCare rewards hospitals for cutting their spending per Medicare beneficiary. The big problem is that the rewards do not distinguish between efficient care and neglectful or stripped-down care.

People pay for ObamaCare once in a monthly premium and then pay more in FICA, Medicare hospital insurance tax if they are employed. The increase in FICA will not be used for Medicare.

Another issue is that hospitals are mandated to sign individuals up for ObamaCare if the patients are uninsured.[325] This can cause issues for people who want to protect their private information or who do not wish to participate in ObamaCare.

Doctors – "You can keep your Doctor" (caveat, caveat, caveat)

The only way a person can keep their doctor is if their medical insurance is qualified insurance under ObamaCare and the particular doctor is in the medical network for coverage or if a person pays the doctor out of pocket without going through the insurance.

The American Medical Association was out front politically endorsing ObamaCare, while doctors were slammed hard by this legislation. Unlike health insurances and the drug companies who get additional money from all the new consumers that enroll in ObamaCare, doctors get millions of new enrollees and a significant pay cut. Not surprisingly, doctors came in second (behind seniors) with dissatisfaction from the legislation.

In order to avoid pay cuts and crushing patient loads, many doctors are retiring early. Many other doctors chose not to participate in ObamaCare and to remain out of the exchange network. Today, three out of ten doctors practice in general medicine.[326] The burden of millions of new patients added by ObamaCare will fall primarily on the "three" doctors, while significantly reducing the pay and the patient load for the "seven" specialty medical doctors. As mentioned earlier, ObamaCare's focus on general medicine doctors is based on the "misconception that Americans overuse specialists and drive up cost in the process."[327] According to Betsy McCaughey, "medical research shows that heart disease patients treated by generalists instead of specialists are often misdiagnosed and treated incorrectly. They are readmitted to the hospital more frequently and die sooner."[328]

Doctors also contend with dilution of their services from the increased hiring of physician assistants and nurse practitioners. The bottom line is that as supply goes down and demand goes up, something has to give. The government allows for either price controls and care rationing, or the health care premium increases.

It is estimated that by 2015 there will be a shortage of more than 60,000 doctors.[329] By 2020, the gap will be a shortage of at least 90,000 doctors, and 130,000 by 2025.[330] There are not enough medical students to supply the huge and ongoing demand created by ObamaCare.

I personally think that doctors or medical students with student loans have a strong argument for breach of contract under a force majeure or contractual interference type of argument. The theory would be something like, had the government not directly interfered with their income potential, they could have paid their student loans. Had students anticipated that health care would become socialized and their income potential would be halved, they would never have entered into the agreement to become a doctor or incur ten years of significant student loan debt. Another issue with being a medical student, (discussed above under Discrimination) keeps students from disadvantaged areas from practicing elsewhere.[331]

Section 6301 creates the Patient-Centered Outcomes Research Institute that studies, recommends, and reports on medical treatments, procedures, drugs and medical devices.[332] Section 3403 creates the IPAB board with all its Medicare cost-cutting power that will certainly be felt by doctors.

Section 3002 helps protect the quality of treatment for Medicare patients; it calls for a lot of reports and compliance measures.

Some of those compliance measures come from more bureaucracy such as electronic health records on patients. Gone are the days of paper. In 2009, the seeds for top-down government control were inserted into the American Recovery and Reinvestment Act by requiring doctors and hospitals to digitize medical health records.[333] Now, in 2015, doctors will be penalized 1.5% of their Medicare reimbursement if they fail to submit a long list of health measurements on their patients.[334] The medical data interfaces with the United Nations medical data records.

Doctors take the Hippocratic Oath to become a doctor. Many, if not all states, reflect in licensing requirements that doctors must maintain their independent judgment in treating patients. ObamaCare makes this especially difficult, especially when limited by constrained budgets, thinning formularies, arbitrary treatment guidelines designed to cut cost and not necessarily for the patient's best interests. ObamaCare says that doctors only are paid if they are in a qualified plan, which follow specific government guidelines. At some point, a doctor may face the decision to do what is best for the patient or face stiff penalties from the government.

A related issue is the cost of malpractice insurance. Moreover, the threat of increased litigation increases medical costs because doctors must practice defensive medicine. This means extra costs for patient tests and procedures to prove that there is no malpractice if the patient develops complications and is injured from advice or treatment.

The Medicare Payment Advisory Commission (MPAC) working in tandem with the IPAB, was established to cut $500 billion out of Medicare. The first places they cut were doctor reimbursements. Specialists' fees are cut 6% per year for three years and frozen at that level for the seven years after that. This effectively gives specialist doctors a 50% real pay cut for accepting Medicare patients.[335]

General practitioners have a 10-year freeze in their pay from Medicare.[336]

One of the lower blows the administration has done was to publicize Medicare Physician payment data out of context. In order to bill Medicare, a doctor has to be on the premises. The physician associated with payment doesn't receive that amount of payment because there is staff, equipment, technical fees, and other costs that come out of that amount. Interestingly, they did not publish the payment data for hospital paid physicians. One of the reasons that this distorted information was released by the Center for Medicare Services in that format was to start generating public bias against how much physicians were paid so that the government could justify to the public the reduction in physician payments.[337]

The costs associated with billing health insurances are staggering:

> Claims and billing ate up the largest portion, 55 percent, of time physicians' practices spent interacting with health insurers. For primary-care practices, it accounted for about 53 percent. Clerical staff spent the largest number of hours on claims and billing, spending an average, per week, of 27.1 hours in primary-care practices, 29.8 hours in medical specialists' practices, and 28.7 hours in surgical specialists' practices.
>
> For small, one-to-two physician practices, the annual cost of dealing with health insurers was greater for primary-care physicians than medical or surgical specialists. Small primary-care practices spent an average of $72,675 interacting with health insurers. Medical specialists spent $70,788 and surgical specialists spent $61,187. The clerical staff, which accounted for the bulk of the hours spent on claims and billing, cost small primary-care practices an average of $31,666 annually, while they cost medical specialists $27,595 and surgical specialists $27,977. The data strongly suggests that primary-care

practices could save substantial time and money by reducing if not eliminating billing expenses.[338]

One issue that the AMA is worried about is contained in Section 1412. Consumers have a "90 day grace period before their subsidized plan is canceled for nonpayment. But insurers only have to keep paying doctors and hospitals for 30 days."[339] What that means is that doctors will eat the cost of treatment received in a 60-day window where the patient has not paid but the insurance is still valid.

The bottom line is that if doctors want to be paid and they are in the ObamaCare system, they will not be treated well. Doctors face lower pay, much higher patient loads, more bureaucracy, higher fines, and less doctors available to spread the load.

Propoganda

I wish I could use the term "advertising" but ads that are full of government lies falls more correctly under the term of "shameless, taxpayer-funded propaganda." The big carriers of this campaign are news media, television, the internet, and our children. The Liberals and Democrats who passed ObamaCare are doing everything they can to "prove" to the public that ObamaCare is working efficiently and the public loves the new health care. That way the lambs will enroll, especially the young, healthy ones. The other types of propaganda are to discredit whistleblowers or justify reductions in programs like Medicare. It is one thing if that were true, it is quite another when it could not be further from the truth. According to data compiled from federal and state sources, the Associated Press found that publicity, marketing and advertising for ObamaCare was $684 million per year.[340]

I talked earlier about the administration beating the drums to get 7 million people to enroll through the exchanges. It was interesting to watch the numbers continue to rise despite the reality to the contrary. The administration was willing to say anything to make those numbers rise and in the end, they just made stuff up to further their political agenda.

For instance, the U.S. Census changed its formula for determining health coverage rates this year.[341] The questions are so different, that it will be impossible to compare the current health care results with the older health care results.[342] I'm sure everyone will be shocked when the Census finds that there is a huge decrease in uninsured citizens. Not surprisingly, this information is expected to be released in September, a few months before the elections.[343]

As discussed under the doctor section above, one of the lower blows the administration has done was to publicize Medicare physician payment data out of context.[344] This was a preliminary strike to get the public to accept the massive cuts in Medicare doctor payments.

Valerie Jarrett, Obama's right hand person, said that the administration was trying to enlist the help of popular sports figures. Other ideas from Ogilvy Public Relations Worldwide is to target Hollywood by getting several popular shows like "Modern Family" or "Grey's Anatomy" to write ObamaCare into the script for some of the $237 million advertising fund grants that went to the exchange.[345] Saturday Night Live had an ObamaCare skit parodying Obama kissing Justin Bieber.[346] A Health care.gov sign was featured prominently with a busty Betty Boop pose from Kim Kardashian.[347]

Even Obama himself has used propaganda to justify ObamaCare. In the 2008 debates, he said, "For my mother to die of cancer at the age of 53 and have to spend the last months of her life in the hospital room arguing with insurance companies because they're saying that this may be a pre-existing condition and they don't have to pay her treatment, there's something fundamentally wrong about that."[348] Yet the truth according to Janny Scott, a New York Times reporter, is that Stanley Ann Dunham was never denied coverage for her disease.[349] Cigna paid for her cancer treatment and met all its contractual obligations. The actual dispute was about a separate disability insurance policy. Another, more amusing propaganda attempt is a picture by the Associated Press of Obama with 13 Obamacare supporters standing behind the podium he was speaking at. What they didn't say was that only three of those people had actually signed up. Or consider that when the President tried to sign up for Obamacare to publicize that he was willing to participate in his own program, but the healthcare.gov website could not verify his identity.[350]

A $1.1 million dollar grant is being used to collect Obamacare success stories.[351]

Particularly cringe-worthy is the conscription of children for propaganda purposes. There is $43 million going towards training 2500 California public school and college students to sell ObamaCare to the public through out-reach calls and "adult-student class presentations."[352] According to *Covered California*,

> "The goal of the grant program is to increase awareness about the new benefits, to educate targeted audiences about the subsidy programs available to them and to motivate consumers and small businesses to be part of obtaining health insurance."[353]

The Los Angeles Unified School District obtained almost $1 million of that grant money. Some of this funding will be used to "train public school staff how to call the parents and guardians of students and urge their enrollment in the *Affordable Care Act* scheme."[354] Class time is approved for this project to teach teenagers about ObamaCare.[355]

The internet campaign as of March 2011 had spent over $1.4 million dollars on pay-per-click online advertising with search engines like Google and Yahoo to funnel searches for ObamaCare.[356] According to Chris Beakey, Vice President of Ogilvy PR Worldwide,

> "You want to utilize the bulk of their paid media efforts (which would include expenditures for Radio One and Univision) on media that reaches African Americans and Hispanics. The money will go farther and these audiences continue to be a top priority."[357]

As part of the push to appeal to young people, go to http://doyougotinsurance.com/ to see all the ads of youngsters partying with alcohol. And a mom skateboarding in high heels with her two sons, really? Young men get bro-surance while they surround the keg of beer, while young women get buddy insurance while they take whiskey shooters off skis or sip wine while working out. Michelle Obama, echoing the media propaganda, appeared on the Tonight show with Jimmy Fallon saying:

> "Young people really needed Obamacare because they are "knuckleheads. . . A lot of young people think they're invincible, but the truth is young people are knuckleheads," she said. Then she indicated that they often cut themselves while cooking or injure themselves by dancing on bar stools.[358]

Women are also a target group. USA Today reports that a multi-million dollar advertising push by Enroll America, an Obamacare advocacy group, will use cats, dogs, birds and other pets to get young women to sign up for health care coverage.[359]

One of the inescapable conclusions is that there is a lot of taxpayer money being spent to brainwash a lot of people. If ObamaCare was so good for everyone, there wouldn't be such public resistance to signing up for it. The other take home lesson is that the administration is counting on the American public to be either apathetic or truly stupid to swallow this mass manipulation. It reminds me of the book discussed below by Andy Andrews, *How do you kill 11 million of people?*[360] The answer: You lie to them! Brainwashing the children is so low it is scraping below the bottom of the barrel.

Oh, You're Just Paranoid!

I ran across a provocatively title book called, *How do you Kill 11 Million People? Why the Truth Matters More than you Think* by Andy Andrews. The short answer is to lie to them like Hitler lied to the Jewish people: "How fortunate for leaders," Hitler said to his inner circle, "that men do not think.

Make the lie big, make it simple, keep saying it, and eventually they will believe it."[361]

One particularly instructive story involved a large Polish, Jewish ghetto. At first, the people were segregated there by poverty and their faith. Walls were put around the ghetto. Then the Jews were told they couldn't leave because it was for their own safety. Then the walls got even higher, with authorities still telling them it was for their safety to keep others out. All the while, the Rabbi leaders were assured that the Germans heard them and that their concerns were in the process of legally being heard, that these matters take time . . . Then the Kristallnacht happened. The Jewish men, women, and children were rounded up, shoved on trains, and promised they were being taken to a better place. Later they were stripped of their belongings and clothes. Then they were herded like animals into gas chambers. That was in the beginning of the Nazi genocide policy that killed 11 million Jews.

Hindsight says this never should have happened and even now, it is unthinkable that someone would get away with this. But there were signs before Hitler came to power. A fringe fascist movement had wormed its way into the political majority. The SS kept their true motive and identity secret from the public. The moral is that outrageous things can happen when people are deceived, they do not question authority, or they remain apathetic. Unscrupulous leaders can make many people do what they normally wouldn't do without a fight. A revolution can happen with small numbers of people. Germany had a population of 79.7 million at the time. The mass genocide happened with only 10% of Germany's population actively working to change the system.[362] The parallels between Germany and in the U.S. government today at this time are uncanny. We need to pay attention to history so we are not doomed to repeat it.

Consider how new ideas are propagated prior to becoming mainstream. They come up first usually in science fiction, like Star Trek, Star Wars or Twenty Thousands Leagues under the Sea. If ideas can be dreamed, in the right circumstances and with the right people, these dreams can become reality. For instance, light and electricity advances from Edison and Tesla were once laughed at by science and were thought to be a fringe area. Now they are a part of our everyday reality and society would have trouble living without these remarkable discoveries. Likewise, many of the fringe ideas we see today will spread to become reality. That is why I like to pay attention to fringe areas. These ideas are news or alerts of what can happen in the future.

What *has* happened? Obama has, so far, unilaterally granted himself martial law power over highways, seaports, communication, highways, electrical power, gas, all forms of energy, cars (including your own personal vehicle), health, education, welfare, airports, railroads, mechanisms of production and distribution, wages, credit, and money.[363] That means that if Obama declares a national state of emergency, he has access to the powers he granted himself via the executive orders he has signed. These executive orders provide that nobody can interfere with Obama for 6 months, **not even Congress**. This is a fact and not fantasy or speculation.

These orders include the power to relocate citizens to any number of the hundreds of FEMA camps that are being revamped for future use.[364] This is also a fact.

Out of Indiana comes a story about labor camps being constructed or revamped for those who don't pay or can't pay ObamaCare penalties.[365] First off, enforcement of ObamaCare penalties comes from the IRS. Their power, at this point, is limited since the penalty is more of an infraction fine and is not a criminal offense. On the other hand, why would an Amtrak railcar facility be upgraded to a labor camp and why would employees say this? Is there anything that substantiates why the same conversions are happening in Arizona, Arkansas, Colorado and California? These camps are expected to open after elections in early 2015. Additional information is:

> Photographic and video evidence shows facilities to be equipped with large 3-4 inch gas mains that are connected to large furnaces, which may function as

> crematoriums. Also seen are several helicopter landing pads, red-blue-green zones for classifying and processing incoming personnel, one way turnstiles, barracks, towers and electrified fences fitted with razor wire to prevent escape.[366]

Many people speculate that an economic crisis from the fall of the U.S. dollar would precipitate such social unrest that order could only be maintained by declaring a national state of emergency, otherwise known as martial law.

There are many government agencies, and not just Homeland Security in the process of buying guns, machine guns, and ammunition. Homeland Security purchased 1.5 billion rounds of bullets in 2012.[367] Over the next 4 or 5 years since that time, they bought another 1.6 billion rounds of ammunition.[368] While some people speculated that this large amount of ammunition was to suppress civil unrest, others speculated it was merely to reduce the supply of ammunition for lawful gun owners. On the other hand, there are others who say the number of bullets purchased are widely exaggerated since the purchase occurs over a number of years.

Although much of the ACA reads like riddles and agendas, there are a couple of inescapable conclusions after reading all 906 pages of ObamaCare. Just about every section requires one or more reports, that it creates an impressive amount of bureaucracy.

Another in-your-face trend is the amount of power transferred from doctors and the medical establishment to the government. A lot of personal choice over individual health care decisions also goes to the government.

Lastly, there is an enormous amount of unaccounted money written into ObamaCare. The costs don't add up. I went through and added up the amount of appropriations allocated by ObamaCare. The costs are supposed to add up to around $1 trillion dollars. I could only find around $138 billion dollars. See, Appendix C. What happened to the other $850 billion dollars? ObamaCare seems to be a very large income transfer from the citizens of the U.S. to someone or funding someone's agenda because it isn't budgeted to go to health care, the government, or paying down the deficit.

As Andrews says, "You see, the danger to America is not a single politician with ill intent. Or even a group of them. The most dangerous thing any nation faces is a citizenry capable of trusting a liar to lead them."[369]

Implantation of RFID chips (Is this true?)

There is a strong Christian base in Louisiana. One question on the minds of Christians is the "mark of the beast" as described in the Bible. The idea of RFID chips has caused a lot of concern about the end times predicted in Revelations.

Microchipping was one area I did a lot of searching to see if it was true or could be true. I couldn't find where it was enacted into law, incorporated into HR 3950, or the corresponding Reconciliation Act HR 4872. So, much of the hype seems to be premature.

However, what I did find does have the potential for government abuse under the right circumstances. Back in 2007, Congress passed legislation directing the FDA to establish a unique identification for Class II medical devices. It wasn't until 2012, after ObamaCare was passed, that the legislation was revisited. Under HR 3200, the idea was resurrected, but with a twist. Instead of just having medical devices identified, they wanted to have the entire medical history of a person embedded in their arm. According to the drafters, this was for our safety. That way a few people would not be able to get additional narcotics from different doctors; in emergencies, doctors would have information about their patients who were otherwise unconscious, and everyone would always have their medical files available wherever they went. Although HR 3200 was never passed, the idea still keeps coming up in successive legislation. Eventually, with persistence and the right circumstances, this will pass like ObamaCare did, unless voters keep this kind of legislator out of office.

What is interesting about the VeriChip is that the technology exists. The chip is about the size of a grain of rice.[370] ObamaCare is obsessed with digitizing medical information, but why stop there? This initiative did not start with President Obama. President Bush was also pushing for digitized medical records. It is only a small leap from digitized medical records, to finding places to store the information. Currently, even the United Nations is working on a project to digitize medical information on a global scale and the U.S. system can interface with that system. In 2004, the ID chip acts like a portal. Every time it is scanned, any information is updated to a master database in a government computer. Now, it may be possible to store the information directly on the chip with periodic uploads to the master record.

Contained in those medical records can be your banking information, entire medical history, where you live, where you work, voter registration, who your family and friends are. The list is extensive and it would follow you everywhere you went or where you will go in the future. Some people have suggested that the chip could replace any plastic card we currently use. There has even been talk that it would be easy to hide a chip like that in food. Although, that begs the question of why it wouldn't pass all the way through the digestive tract?

I was talking to my friend, Terri Estay. She told me that an elderly lady from her church in Galliano, Louisiana, had received a letter about putting a microchip in her right hand. It was optional and for her convenience. Galliano is a very small town in the country and in a non-participating exchange state. My guess is the RFID push is more developed than we think if they can reach people in obscure places of the country.

So, yes, it is possible that Big Brother could use a personal RFID Chip to keep track of you and everything about you. As history shows, it would start small and voluntarily "for your safety" or "for you convenience" and then get progressively mandatory with more types of information stored on the chip, until it is illegal to be without the chip.

Luckily for legal gun owners, the National Rifle Association (NRA) was there at the time this legislation was crafted. Because of them, specific rights were protected in section 2716. The government has unconstitutionally been trying to infringe on gun ownership for some time now. On the ObamaCare wish list was a national database that inventoried all the guns, ammunition, owners, and etc. The NRA inserted a provision that keeps ObamaCare from trying to collect this information, affecting premiums, coverage, or having gun ownership as a factor any decisions by the IAPB.

People concerned with gun rights should be aware that grandfathered insurance plans do not need to comply with these ObamaCare regulations.

The law gets a little muddy when anti-gun agendas abound. We've seen some health care providers who continue to try to get gun information. In fact, on January 15, 2013, Obama issued 23 executive orders, many of them gun-related. One of them was to clarify that the ACA does not prohibit doctors from asking patients about guns in their homes.[371] Legal gun owners do not have to give any information to them under ObamaCare.

In the news, we've seen stories about schools trying to pump schoolchildren for gun information in their home "for the safety of the children." Schools are showing out with the leftist agenda through many different vehicles like Common Core, or changing our history books. It is not out of the question that data collection by school nurses, counselors, or teachers could be a potential threat. It is sort of under ObamaCare, but it isn't really. In legal terms, we call this a gray area. Agencies also have unofficial policies for enforcing rules. Who knows what one of those 159 boards or agencies could come up with. Even if it is pure semantics, this is one area that everyone should pay careful attention to and not let them get away with it. Just because it looks like gun owners are protected, it is only a thin layer of protection.

The more interesting cases are that there are NO protections for unlawful ownership of guns and ammunition. This could be problematic in situations like Connecticut or New York where they had a mandatory registration of a certain type of gun. Thousands of citizens refused to register under penalty of civil disobedience because the law was unconstitutional. Veterans with mild or temporary PTSD or other people with mild or temporary psychological symptoms caused from a death in the family, postpartum depression, or an emotional divorce, and who talk to their doctor, could potentially have this reported in their medical records. After the medical records are digitized, it is very easy for any of the 159 agencies or boards to search for a term, put it in a database, and use the information as a way to deny legal gun ownership.

If this was pure paranoia on my part, then why is the ATF trying to change the definition of "adjudicated as a mental defective" in the *Federal Register.* The proposed rule change is to: "clarify that the statutory term 'adjudicated as a mental defective' includes persons who are found incompetent to stand trial or not guilty by reason of mental disease or defect, lack of mental responsibility, or insanity, and that the term includes persons found guilty but mentally ill." According to Michael Connelly of the Constitutional Law Alliance:

> "What is left unstated is what constitutes a 'mental defective.' Under the explanation for the proposed rule provided in the *Federal Register*, it is claimed that the intent of Congress in passing the GCA (Gun Control Act) was so that 'the prohibition against the receipt and possession of firearms would apply broadly to 'mentally unstable' or 'irresponsible' persons.' Even assuming that this interpretation of Congressional intent were correct, there is no definition of the term "irresponsible," leaving it up to a variety of individuals and institutions to add anyone to NICS [database list].[372]

Since there is a wide sharing of medical information allowed between the different agencies, there could be some large issues here. It looks like people who do not legally have a gun or are judged as "irresponsible" could be subject to not only being recorded in a national database but subjected to higher premiums or denied eligibility into health-related or other wellness programs.

Privacy

Legally speaking, a person has the right to be let alone, meaning the "right of a person to withhold himself and his property from public scrutiny if he so chooses."[373] The issue of privacy is a derived fundamental constitutional right. In other words, it wasn't expressly granted in the Constitution or the Bill of Rights, but rather it was an implied right. A lot of privacy law developed as a tort and provided a remedy for breach of privacy in four types of circumstances where the release of private information was harmful: (1) Public Disclosure of Private and Embarrassing Facts, (2) False Light, (3) Intrusion and (4) Misappropriation.

The constitutional right of privacy is about how much personal information the government is entitled to get from you and under what circumstances. Generally, the government can have access to your personal information if the government can prove a compelling interest. These interests include psychological health, public morality, and improving the quality of life.[374]

Congress has also passed many different laws that restrain corporations, financial institutions, the medical community, the legal profession, and many other areas of our lives that people could use our personal information against us. The Privacy Act of 1974 prevents the federal government from releasing your private information without your permission or as otherwise authorized by law.[375]

The government constantly increases their sphere of information gathering, which can be a gauge for how they will treat confidential information received from enrollees in ObamaCare. The first step is to blur the lines between public and private. Consider the new White House Internet

Privacy Policy via the new Office of Digital Security. The government considers that anything on the internet is public information, including the date, time and duration of online visits and the originating internet protocol address.[376] Also consider how wide-reaching this policy is:

> "Obama's online strategy now includes a *We the People* petitions platform, live online chats and more than a dozen social media sites including Google Plus, LinkedIn, Pinterest, Instagram, Vine, MySpace and seven different Facebook pages including La Casa Blanca and Education to Innovate. Visitors who link to those social media sites are advised: 'Your activity on those sites is governed by the third-party website's security and privacy policies,' which frequently allow those companies to sell users' data. In addition, the White House archives Twitter, Facebook and Google Plus content to comply with the Presidential Records Act."[377]

This means that any time you go to certain websites, everything is recorded whether it is naughty, nice, or conservative. Sometimes it might be as quick as a cookie inserted in your web browser and recording your internet address, other times it is a record of a full online chat. What is certain is that this information isn't just going to be used to see if third-party websites are complying with the Presidential Records Act. If the government keeps a record, they will use it for any government purpose under the rubric of "public information."

One of the most intimate issues requiring privacy is our personal medical records. Turning that information over to 159 agencies and boards who share that information with each other does not lend itself to privacy. As discussed earlier, there is a large push to get digitized medical information and not only a national health database to put all this information in, but eventually a global health database.

Another narrowly-construed category of privacy is through the Fourteenth Amendment under a due process clause.

The government cannot take away your liberty of actions or decisions regarding family, marriage, procreation, or motherhood. Theoretically, the due process clause should protect your autonomous right to decide birth control issues. Ergo, government should not be able to dictate to insurances that they must cover birth control. This is because birth control is a personal choice and that there is no compelling reason to force this policy onto the people. This due process privacy issue should protect more than just bedroom matters.

Now let's look at how ObamaCare directly could be or already has been used to violate privacy. The amount of sharing of everyone's personal information with such a large government entity is ripe for abuse, intentional or unintentional. There are issues with collection, storage, hiring, vendettas, and control of patient behaviors.

For instance, ObamaCare records want to include more than just medical information, like banking or relationship information. The RFID chip discussed above, could tie your personal data to other records like shopping habits, where you travel, and whom you see. There is nothing that the government would not know about you. Consequently, the issue of privacy is a very BIG deal when it concerns the government.

ObamaCare grants some large powers on intra-agency sharing. There are several mentioned agencies to share information with and "other entities as determined appropriate by the Secretary."[378] Furthermore, certain data is shared with non-governmental entities according to their data disclosure agreements that are deemed appropriate by the Secretary.[379]

One privacy issue under ObamaCare is that businesses become an enforcer too. In order for business to determine if they are compliant with government regulations, they must find out and report household income to the government. How comfortable are people reporting household income to their boss? In some households, it may not matter. But in other households, especially if a member is looking to the boss for a raise, it could be crucial information that biases a boss against giving a raise.

Another issue concerned patient navigators. Apparently, there are no background checks required for employees working as an ObamaCare Navigator.[380] Any terrorist or criminal could have a field day with your personal information contained in the file, sell it, or use it as blackmail.

One of the ObamaCare Myths, addressed on the government website, has to do with the security of the website. They claim that the website is totally secure,[381] while on the other hand, hackers are able to take sensitive private information, including bank data, social security and your birthdate.[382] Thus, it makes it easy for identity theft to occur.

Vindictive agencies "leak" personal information with no accountability. We've seen both, the IRS and DOJ, used as swords against people who oppose Obama. Here's a new privacy issue. Although Facebook is considered a private actor, an unexplainable glitch leaked a helper's personal eBenefit account. What happened? Lauren Price is the Public Affairs representative for a veteran's advocacy group named "Veteran Warriors." She was helping a veteran of Desert Storm, Iraq, and Afghanistan with his GI bill application. They were using Facebook private messaging since the veteran did not have access to a telephone. When he logged in under his personal eBenefits account with his unique personal user name and password, he was given access to Lauren's eBenefits account. At no time did she ever give this to the veteran or make it available to him in their private messaging. The conclusion is that there was some kind of retaliation from the Veterans Administration (VA) against Lauren for being an outspoken advocate against the VA that also involved Facebook.[383]

A public (or so we thought) entity working with the government and used for retaliation purposes should make people wonder 1) if that much control of our personal information belongs in the hands of the government, and 2) just how secure is our information really? The Veterans

Administration is only one small agency that will interface with all the other Agencies and boards of ObamaCare.

How would they control you? One example is if you can you imagine the Secretary determining you or a member of your family as overweight. Then the person's name is put into a national database to control your behavior. The person can only purchase approved food or the store scanner goes beeeeeep! And everyone turns to look. Or perhaps the person gets fined every time they miss a wellness program appointment? Sounds like a 1984 moment, but how far would health care go to control you, your behavior, and your family? They have death counselling for Medicare recipients every 5 years, so what wellness mandate might they order for overweight people?

Or how many people want information shared if they have a history of depression, AIDS, or some other sexually transmitted disease? Would the government round people up and put them in one spot to make it less expensive to care for them? Don't say it can't happen because Germany did this for people needing long-term care. They sent the old folks over to Africa because it was cheaper to care for them there.

The bottom line is that personal information is and can be used for controlling you and your behavior. Information is power. Autonomy decisions should be protected so that individuals can have choices on the most intimate areas of their lives. Autonomy could include personal liberty to be left alone, not monitored or controlled such as where people travel, shop, or what they buy.

Contraception/Abortion

Abortion is a hot-button to begin with, but buried in the ObamaCare legislation is the end run around the reproductive-control resistance by mandating that insurances pay for contraception. The Roman Catholics, in particular, consider this an infringement on the First Amendment, freedom of religion constitutionally guaranteed right.

Under section 1303(1), states are granted the right to prohibit abortion coverage in plans offered through an exchange.[384] Moreover, health care providers or health care facilities cannot be forced to provide coverage or referrals for abortion.[385]

The Supreme Court heard arguments on the *Hobby Lobby* case on April 29, 2014.[386] The question before the court was whether a contraceptive mandate by the government violates the free exercise of religion of a family owned business or closely-held business organization. There has been no decision as yet, but early questioning by the court seemed to center around the issue of whether a family business is a person entitled to protection by the constitution. The court seemed to be leaning towards the idea that a business is not constitutionally protected regarding religious matters. This is a bit ironic since *Citizen's United* allows corporations to be counted as a person for political contribution purposes.[387]

One pointed question asked of the government's attorney was if he realized that the logical conclusion of his reasoning would mean that the government could mandate abortion? He answered along the lines, yes, but the government doesn't intend to go that far. Nothing will be known for sure until the official opinion comes out by the Supreme Court.

Everything Hinges on the Vote

Considering all the executive powers that Obama has granted himself, he easily could create a situation that would make 2014 the last election. Since he would have six months of unfettered access to control power, energy, military, money, and people in the case of a national emergency, he would have plenty of time to take care of Congress and any opposition to his plans. In order to make that a reality, it would be helpful to have a democratically controlled Senate and House so the power grab isn't so obvious. That way, they could continue making laws that would help him with becoming the first dictator of the United States.

Congress needs to represent the people. Congress needs to put strict boundaries on the creation of Executive Orders. There needs to be accountability for those people who not only failed to protect the Constitution pursuant to their sworn oaths, but who actively tried to dismantle the Constitution and the U.S. This isn't a partisan statement, because I think there are people in both parties who fit into this category.

ObamaCare needs to be repealed, not tweaked. The law is so bad and so enormous, that people are still finding out what stink-bombs it contains. I am skeptical about the "replace" crowd because RomneyCare started as a Republican vision and the Democratic ObamaCare was based on RomneyCare. There is no way to tweak the ACA because it is so pervasive and overreaching in controlling the medical field and the nation.

The three greatest threats in voting are, 1) voter fraud/intimidation; 2) an insane amount of money available for campaigning with funding for incessant, hard-hitting brain-washing ads in swing states, and 3) electronic voting.

It should be common sense that one registered voter gets one vote. There may have been a time where voter ID may not have been necessary, but when voter fraud is so prevalent, we need to be able to verify that people are United States citizens and that they are properly registered to vote.

How are people supposed to consider a vote valid when there are more dead people, pets, and undocumented aliens voting than registered voters? Or when people vote numerous times like it was American Idol instead of a national vote? Consider that people were receiving voter-ID-premarked-as-Democrat applications when they signed up for health care through ObamaCare Exchanges. Don't forget that the DOJ allowed the Black Panthers to intimidate voters at the polls without any repercussions.

Voter ID laws and voter security at the polls are crucial to preventing fraud and ensuring that the outcome of the vote is the majority will of the people. We need to have accountability of all the government branches so that there are no unconstitutional voter manipulations like a national interstate compact pledging to vote for the national popular vote winner regardless of how their own state votes.[388] If people are going to be railroaded into a popular vote instead of the electoral vote, then above all else, the vote needs to be fair and real.

In 2008, Ohio was saturated with political awards of government contracts to sway voters to vote for Obama and the Democratic Party candidates. Ohio was saturated with media coverage, bought and paid for with the use of foreign funds (disguised as coming from legitimate sources), large corporation donations (courtesy of the Supreme Court decision in *Citizens United*), or big lobby interests (insurance and pharmacy). A leftover from the days of FDR, it is unfair for taxpayers of all 50 states to have to pay for the state contracts of a couple of swing states, especially when politically motivated to swing votes. Most of the heavy interests and funding were in favor of Obama.

Either there should be strict anti-hacking controls, verified by many different sources, on electronic voting or dual voting so there is a paper copy for verification if needed. When George W. Bush was elected, there were suspicions of fraud because of the number of last-minute votes he received. The same thing happened in 2012 with Obama. Electronic countermeasures verifying authentic votes are crucial, especially if some states are trying to change to a popular vote instead of the Electoral College.

ObamaCare represents the largest tax increase, transfer of power, and transfer of money to the government that we have seen since the founding of our nation in 1776. Since controlling health care is the cornerstone to creating a communist country, voting is important to prevent the end of the "great experiment" envisioned by the Founding Fathers from being dismantled by the "great swindle" of communism.

People need to remain vigilant to keep their constitutionally protected rights or they will lose them, one by one. They need to break out of their apathetic shell and pay attention so that a Hitler-esque leader never comes to the U.S. Look at where the power goes by tracing the money. Since many waivers and deadline extensions occur prior to elections, the powers that be are looking to win elections, so democracy is still a part of the plan, for now. However, the same could be said of Hitler too. He needed to win his election so he could dismantle the government into a dictatorship.

Many of you might be wondering what does all this have to do with ObamaCare? Earlier I talked about following the power and money with ObamaCare. Taking over the health care industry is one of the first things that dictators do prior to assuming total control of a government. Hitler, Stalin, Lenin, Castro, Mussolini, all of these people knew that control of health care was a cornerstone for their plan. Whether this happens in the U.S. remains to be seen. This is still a fringe concept that could happen under the right circumstances.

To reiterate a point, Kristallnacht happened because it was easier for the Jews to believe the lies that they were told by their government. All of the reasons we were told that ObamaCare was passed and explanations for the glitches from implementation of ObamaCare have been lies. At the very least, given the above history, people should be informed, demand accountability from their government, and insist that those executive orders be declared illegal. That means voting for the proper people who will vote properly to protect the people and Constitution of the United States.

Solutions

My bachelor's degree is in Communication. One of the models for problem solving is to brainstorm. I'm going to throw out a lot of ideas to get the ball rolling, some obviously better than others. For a free medical system to survive, it needs to be able to think outside of the box and truly solve the core problems inherent in the system. But the crucial take home message is that there are health care options other than Obamacare.

One of the best books around for advice for a business to survive chaotic and uncertain times is written by Jim Collins,

Great by Choice: Uncertainty, Chaos, and Luck--Why Some Thrive Despite Them All. I believe that it also provides a model to fix the health industry and allow Medicare and Medicaid to thrive without developing into trillion dollar unfunded mandates. One of the largest problems is that Obamacare is too large and seeks to wipe out several unfunded mandates at the expense of people who have paid into the system for years. So, it isn't just about health care, it is also about the national budget, controlling U.S. citizens, power, and syphoning off big money to a few elites.

The worst thing a business can do is to strip everything down and begin with new personnel, and new directions, while expanding the old business model the whole time. It is like a shotgun approach with no real direction. These businesses virtually failed 100% of the time.

The best way to survive is to "observe what worked, figured out why it worked, and build upon proven foundations. 10X companies were the group that thrived under the adverse conditions. The 10X companies were not more risk taking, more bold, more visionary, and more creative than the comparison companies. The 10Xers were more disciplined, more empirical, and more paranoid."[389] These companies had leaders who had the three top behaviors: fanatic discipline, empirical creativity, and productive paranoia.[390]

According to Jim Collins,

> "Discipline, in essence, is consistency of action—consistency with values, consistency with long-term goals, consistency with performance standards, consistency of method, consistency over time. True discipline requires the independence of mind to reject pressures to conform in ways incompatible with values, performance standards, and long-term aspirations. For a 10Xer, the only legitimate form of discipline is self discipline, having the inner will to do whatever it takes to create a great outcome, no matter how difficult.[391]

Empirical creativity is a method and behavior that observes various cause and effect scenarios and applies a creative solution based on the solution or solutions that can cover as many of those uncertain situations as possible.[392] In many ways, by hedging their bets, these companies are able to remain stable. While paranoia may have a bad connotation, productive paranoia is actually a very good thing. These are the people that can see any number of dangers on the horizon and because they are attuned to solving the what-ifs, they are able to steer their company in a way that can minimize dangers and keep the company stable.[393]

Other qualities of 10x companies were that it was not enough to be successful; these companies measured themselves by impact, contribution and purpose.[394] Collins and his team analyzed over 87,000 companies for the cash-to asset ratio. The 10x companies carried 3-10 times more cash to assets for their ratio. [395] These companies would plan an operating agenda that was specific, methodical, and consistent.[396]

This plan is called a SMaC recipe by Collins:

> When formulating a SMaC recipe, ask, "What durable and specific practices best drive our results?" In laboratory working sessions with executives, we've employed the following methodology: 1. Make a list of successes your enterprise has achieved. 2. Make a list of disappointments your enterprise has experienced. 3. What specific practices correlate with the successes but not the disappointments? 4. What specific practices correlate with the disappointments but not the successes? 5. Which of these practices can last perhaps ten to thirty years and apply across a wide range of circumstances? 6. Why do these specific practices work? 7. Based on the above, what SMaC recipe, consisting of 8 to 12 points that reinforce each other as a coherent system, best drives your results?[397]

Any changes to this plan would be one element or aspect at a time, which ensures that the good parts of the company plan remains stable while watching what happens when exploring growth or a potential direction change prior to making a large commitment or investment that can kill the company. The 10X companies changed their plan about 15% while other companies changed over 60%.[398] "Uncontrollable risks are those that expose the enterprise to forces and events that it has little ability to manage or control."[399]

For instance, ObamaCare was supposedly enacted to cover 3.5 million people. Take a billion dollars to cover them. Then take a trillion dollars and cover people who have cancer or heart surgery so they don't lose their homes. Both solutions are much simpler and cheaper than Obamacare. Three other simple solutions are 1) change the incentives for what Medicare will pay for; 2) allow insurances to go across state lines; and 3) stop mandating what all insurance plans will cover. All of these are simple solutions that won't cost the nation $220 trillion dollars and they are very easy to implement without disrupting a SMaC plan.

Here are some ideas that could help change our health care and make it a model for the rest of the world. When considering these ideas, remember to keep the model consistent with small changes to any plan and make sure enough cash on reserve keeps the system afloat. Obviously, some will be better than others will and easier to implement than others.

Seniors

We could create centers that specialize in senior issues because it is much cheaper to keep seniors from being disabled than to pay for long-term care. It would be cost effective for Medicare to pay for a community senior center that specializes in procedures that concern seniors, such as unclogging arteries, replace worn out hips and knees, and remove cataracts. Cancer specialists could also be a part of these centers.

Perhaps there could be an additional research program attached to this for heart disease, cancer, and Alzheimer's.

If we can identify who is susceptible and how to prevent them from occurring, that would save more money than it would cost for the initial research facilities.

In home health services and access to community-based care is cheaper than hospitalization. Therefore, make more money available for home health services and reduce incentives to hospitalize seniors if at all possible without harming their quality care. This will also help keep seniors from being exposed to additional, harmful bacteria and viral infections that can be found in hospitals.

Low-cost Medical for the Expensive Procedures.

There is no reason for someone to lose their home or have to file for bankruptcy for costly medical procedures. As a nation, we could create a pool of money to be used towards paying for these procedures outright. I know that makes some people take a deep breath in, but we could do this with a small fraction of the trillions we are paying for ObamaCare. There might even be a way through this mechanism to stimulate lower cost drugs and increase research with the proper controls in place. Using free market principals, removing government cost controls, and cutting out the middleman insurances, we could make this idea economical and feasible.

Businesses

Remove the barriers for small businesses. According to George W. Bush, "Many self-employed Americans couldn't afford health insurance because the tax code disadvantaged them and regulations prohibited small business owners from pooling risk across jurisdictional boundaries."[400] Moreover, self-employed individuals pay for health insurance with post-tax earnings, while big companies can use pre-tax earnings to pay their health insurance.[401]

It makes a lot more sense to give tax breaks to businesses for providing health insurance than to penalize them for not covering employees. That way businesses can provide what they can afford. Businesses will not have to choose between hiring full-time workers or paying penalties to the government.

Hospitals and Doctors

The budgets of hospitals and doctors are maximized to take advantage of certain Medicare payments. They do what they are incentivized to do. Slowly change the items that are incentivized in a way that also reduces costs without harming quality.

Another way to curb costs is tort reform such that malpractice claims are reduced enough that costs for defensive medicine become unnecessary.

Food

Large corporations are the culprits by cost-shifting public health and staggering medical costs in favor of larger corporate profits. Our food is genetically modified and the over-farming reduces the nutritional value of what we eat. Other predators are large corporations who make money by selling us fat-laden foods, sugary foods, and salty foods. Improper nutrition and the fat-sugar-salt trio causes many health issues including obesity, diabetes, hardening of the arteries, and a whole host of nasty diseases.

Instead of putting a Band-Aid on the problem by labeling fast foods and singling out chronic conditions for treatment, we need to go after the growers, sellers, and manufacturers of those foods. Speak their language through tax incentives to do the right thing instead of fines and penalties that obviously are not working.

Food and Drug Administration

It costs the pharmaceuticals an average of 1.3 billion to bring a new drug to the market.[402] Take a second look at the procedure and see what we could do to lower the costs and reduce the time it takes to bring drugs to market. See if there could be a way to put certain drugs on an expedited tract.

HSAs and Universal Tax Credits

It is a great way to encourage people to take responsibility for their medical needs by having a savings account devoted to medical expenses.

Universal tax credits would also provide incentive for everyone to participate in health insurance. Many people would be medically well covered between a HSA and a low-cost, catastrophic coverage health plan.

Concierge medicine

When patients pay a sum certain directly to doctors on a yearly basis to take care of them, this is called concierge medicine. For instance, $1,000 per year would allow a patient to see their doctor whenever and as frequent as they need to. Maybe in groups that have specialists, the amount could be $2,000 for access to all the doctors. Healthy people might see the doctor once or twice a year, so this amount might be unrealistic. The other scenario is the hypochondriacs. Perhaps there could be a three-tier system with an evaluation of the amount every year?

Consider if 500 patients pay $1,500 apiece. That is a gross revenue of $750,000 for the practice. Many concierge doctors also bill Medicare and private insurance for services not covered by their retainer.

The benefit to this system is that ultimately, it costs less money for small practices because they do not have the additional costs of billing insurances.

Sally Pipes Suggestions[403]

Sally Pipes came up with ten principles for a health care reform. While several ideas have already been widely discussed, several remain uniquely hers.

> Promote private ownership within a thriving individual health insurance marketplace.
>
> Make health insurance portable and treat them like private property. Rather than the onus being on businesses to provide health insurance, perhaps the

voucher would be a better option. That way businesses can provide health insurance for their employees and get the tax write off, yet workers will have the autonomy necessary for the coverage to be portable.

Allow individuals and families to buy health insurance with tax-free dollars.

Give doctors and hospitals a tax deduction for charitable care

Scrip

The current monetary system prints money that is not backed by anything of value. The federal government prints money out of thin air and then the banking system charges interest on that money to utilize it. This creates a system where users will never get ahead. Over a long period of time, people go into a state of economic slavery.

However, if a monetary system is backed by people's labor, then the system produces value and economic freedom. There has to be strict controls that keep the scrip issuance honest or it wrecks it for everyone – like when the South was issuing scrip and everyone was printing their own scrip. It became worthless.

What the State can do is to estimate how much it will cost to pay for health care in the State. Then they can issue scrip in that amount and pay costs with scrip. When scrip is used, then it is destroyed to prevent inflation. Scrip would need to be accepted by local businesses as an exchange like money.

The other part of this is to require the federal government to pay in coin only. That way the State gets real money and not baseless pieces of paper.

Vacation medicine

Combine medicine and vacation. Offer an incentive to have people from not only the United States, but all over the world to come to a medical center in the state for an operation and a spa type of vacation for recovery. Have airport shuttles and make medicine part of the hotel hospitality scene.

Anti-Exchange Medicine

Invite doctors and drug companies that have been ousted from ObamaCare states into non-participating states. Use the free market to make health care the premier industry in the state.

Congressional Fixes

No bill over 10 pages and the congressperson must certify that they read and understood the law.

Any bill that is going to affect a significant amount of the GNP must have a 2/3 vote to pass. Early estimates were that ObamaCare affected 20% of GNP, but inflation and implementation costs are much higher than that.

Executive Fixes

No more Czars. Congress needs to curb the authority of creation and scope of executive orders.

Judicial Fixes

Term limits should be mandatory since a lifetime appointment encourages a long time of abuse if any one president stacks the court in their political favor.

Another option could be a popular vote of the people. If there are over 50 percent of the voters that disagree with a Supreme Court decision, then their decision is automatically reversed and the minority decision stands. If there are 60 percent of the voters who disagree with the Supreme Court decision, then those who voted with the majority opinion lose their jobs.

These two provisions would guard against court stacking and there would be accountability to the people. This would also discourage presidents from nominating the more radical judges because there is always that chance their judicial selection could be overridden by popular vote of the people. This would also help to minimize pressure from the

President, blackmail threats from the NSA, or pressure from Congress.

Health Insurance

One of the biggest reasons for premiums being so high is that there is a mandated list of items that must be covered. For instance, women don't need to pay for prostate exams and men don't need to pay for childbearing issues. People would pay a lot less if they could use a menu type of list that allows them to select items they want to be covered for.

Allowing insurance across state lines is a good thing because it allows for greater pooling of resources to take care of more people. On the other hand, that opens up insurance to federal regulation because it is in the realm of interstate commerce. Perhaps a Congressional law that allows for interstate health insurance compacts without too much government interference.

Don't get me wrong, I think there is a place for health insurance. I think that for large companies or small businesses where they can cross-jurisdictional boundaries for pooling rates, this could be good.

On the other hand, when billing requires so much resources, that it significantly drives up the cost of medicine - that is bad. Additionally, while it may be a good way to make money by pooling the risk, as a person ages, the costs get so high that it is hard to afford insurance. Somehow, there needs to be genuine emphasis on "affordable" and not just lip service.

Accountable Care Organizations

This is like the Walmart of health care where all your medical needs are under one roof. The ACO model allows the integrative health delivery systems to cut out the health insurances to keep the profits to themselves. The other option is for health insurances to transform themselves into an ACO by purchasing or entering directly into exclusive agreements with "efficient hospital systems, ACOs or physician groups."[404] In order for these models to keep premium prices down and the quality of care up for consumers, there must be competing market forces. That means there must be several sources that want the business so they are willing to keep their prices down to a competitive level.

Nullification

When the executive, judicial, and legislative branches of government fail to protect the people, the States retain their right as the ultimate arbiter. What types of conditions would spur the States to act? Looking at The Declaration of Independence gives us a clue:

> We hold these truths to be self-evident, that all men are created equal, that they are endowed by their Creator with certain unalienable Rights, that among these are Life, Liberty and the pursuit of Happiness.– That to secure these rights, Governments are instituted among Men, deriving their just powers from the consent of the governed, –That whenever any Form of Government becomes destructive of these ends, it is the Right of the People to alter or to abolish it, and to institute new Government, laying its foundation on such principles and organizing its powers in such form, as to them shall seem most likely to effect their Safety and Happiness. . . .
>
> The history of the present King of Great Britain is a history of repeated injuries and usurpations, all having in direct object the establishment of an absolute Tyranny over these States. To prove this, let Facts be submitted to a candid world. . . .
>
> He has obstructed the Administration of Justice, by refusing his Assent to Laws for establishing Judiciary powers.
> He has made Judges dependent on his Will alone, for the tenure of their offices, and the amount and payment of their salaries.
> **He has erected a multitude of New Offices, and sent hither swarms of Officers to harrass our people, and eat out their substance**. . . .

> **For imposing Taxes on us without our Consent:** ...
>
> For taking away our Charters, abolishing our most valuable Laws, and altering fundamentally the Forms of our Governments: . . .
>
> For suspending our own Legislatures, and declaring themselves invested with power to legislate for us in all cases whatsoever. . . .
>
> In every stage of these Oppressions We have Petitioned for Redress in the most humble terms: Our repeated Petitions have been answered only by repeated injury. A Prince whose character is thus marked by every act which may define a Tyrant, is unfit to be the ruler of a free people. . . .

Total power over health care is not an enumerated power of the federal government written in the Constitution of the United States. Health care and insurance in general have been traditionally matters of the States. In fact, it makes much more sense to administer health care on a state basis because each state has a unique mix of people and different health care needs. For instance, Florida has a higher population of seniors than other states and seniors have many different needs than other populations.

At present, there are many States that have passed various forms of Nullification of various aspects of ObamaCare, such as making it a crime for enforcement of Obamacare penalties within the State.

Voting

I read a great definition of politics. It is getting the other person to pay for what you want. This fits ObamaCare and the states that support it perfectly.

I am very passionate about getting people educated about ObamaCare and then getting them fired up enough to vote so that we can repeal it. Many people ask, "Can't we fix it instead? Why do we need to repeal it?" My answer is that ObamaCare must be repealed. There are 906 pages of

ObamaCare, more than 20,000 pages of DHHS regulations a year ago, and 159 agencies and boards. If that doesn't make your skin crawl, look at how much money has already been spent and allocated. It is around $150 billion. That makes $850 billion that is unaccounted for. Then we can talk about zero privacy, the destruction of health care as we know it, and the inordinate amount of control that ObamaCare has over people and the individual States. The Supreme Court failed the people, showing that the constitutional safeguard of the appeals process does not work with such a politically charged issue. While there can be small fixes to certain items, there is no way to fix these bigger issues other than to repeal the legislation.

There are checks and balances in the Constitution that are supposed to keep the minority safe from the tyranny of the majority. At the time it was passed, I think nobody actually understood ObamaCare so it looked like a majority of the people agreed with the legislation. But in actuality, the Congress did an end-run around the Constitution and passed it without one Republican vote. Every Democrat who is now in favor of Obama or who participated in the sham vote needs to be voted out of office. I also think they should face criminal prosecution for serious misdeeds against the people and failure to uphold their oath of office to uphold the Constitution.

Many voting issues obscure the will of the people. They have to do with campaign financing, voter identification, verification that people are eligible to vote, apathy, and electronic voting.

There needs to be campaign-financing reform so that corporations and foreign nations like the Middle East or China cannot organize or backhandedly affect our politics through donations.

I don't know about you, but I have a problem with people registered to vote in several states, or that dead people and their pets can vote, or people that are not U.S. citizens can vote. Consistent court blockage of any measure to ensure voting accuracy is insanity, undemocratic, and fails to uphold the Constitution they are sworn to protect. While I do understand the arguments that voter ID might pose to some people, I think that when there is such widespread abuse of the voting process that IDs become crucial to reflect the real will of the people.

I also have a problem with electronic voting. There is enough evidence for the past three elections that suggest the vote was stolen at the last minute through hacking and electronic data manipulation.

Theoretically, 11 states have enough electoral votes to win the election.[405] Everyone who is a registered voter should have his or her votes matter. It is wrong to allow groups like the Black Panthers intimidate voters at the polls. It is wrong to pre-mark voter registrations as Democratic. It is wrong to drive invalids to the polls and help them to vote Democrat. It is wrong to exclude the military overseas from voting because they can't get their votes back to the U.S. in time to be counted.

The newest thwarting to voters is the new state compacts. These states pledge their electoral votes to the candidate who is winning the popular vote. Not only is this unconstitutional, but instead of a state vote, we now have regional voting. This means that one state could vote for one candidate and the electoral votes will go to the other candidate because the state is a member of this compact.

One of the biggest ways to ensure a fair vote is by muting the commercials or refusing to watch TV. If you do listen to commercials or newspapers, become informed so you can make an informed decision. The funding behind the commercials/ads will be an assault from those who support ObamaCare and who do not necessarily have the best interests of the people at heart. Hitler is proof of the truism, "If you say it enough, people will believe it." We saw the effect of these hard-hitting brainwashing commercials in Swing states like Florida, Colorado and Ohio with their blitz ad campaigns.

Another way to ensure that voter's voices are properly heard is to educate voters through a massive grass-roots effort and make sure that the voter numbers accurately reflect the will of the people.

Conclusion

There are so many aspects to ObamaCare that it is hard to boil it down to a few pages or speak about it in a short amount of time. When I first started this project, I figured that a paper could be written that would cover twenty to thirty pages. Little did I realize that it would consume a staggering amount of time and blossom into enough material for a book.

If ObamaCare were just about controlling costs, it would be easy to change it and then control Medicare costs. Unfortunately, the scope of the ACA is so large and invasive into the American way of life that we can't afford to allow this leviathan loose. It has already cost millions and millions of dollars and is projected to cost exponentially more. ObamaCare must be repealed. We have no choice.

Please encourage people to read this or go to the website http://icitizenpatriot.com. The materials will be downloadable in a .pdf format, book format, video format, and a kindle format.

Tell your friends. Let's get the word out and Save our Seniors, Save our Medicine, Save our Doctors, Save our Businesses, and Save America! We've got a country to educate and grassroots voters to mobilize!

And always - God Bless America!

APPENDIX A – Health Care Czar Powers

Citizens' Council on Health Care, June 2010
www.cchconline.org

"Secretary"	3267 times
"Secretary shall"	1051 times
"by the Secretary	651 times
"Secretary may"	371 times
"Secretary determines"	222 times
"Secretary under"	80 times
"Secretary in consultation"	39 times

I asked for permission to post the actual chart, but no response.

APPENDIX B – Agencies & Boards

159 Ways the Senate Bill Is a Government Takeover of Health Care

Posted February 25, 2010

Courtesy of the Senate Republican Policy Committee:

Here is a list of new boards, bureaucracies, and programs created in the 2,733 page Senate health care bill, which serves as the framework for President Obama's health proposal:

1. Grant program for consumer assistance offices (Section 1002, p. 37)
2. Grant program for states to monitor premium increases (Section 1003, p. 42)
3. Committee to review administrative simplification standards (Section 1104, p. 71)
4. Demonstration program for state wellness programs (Section 1201, p. 93)
5. Grant program to establish state exchanges (Section 1311(a), p. 130)
6. State American Health Benefit Exchanges (Section 1311(b), p. 131)
7. Exchange grants to establish consumer navigator programs (Section 1311(i), p. 150)
8. Grant program for state cooperatives (Section 1322, p. 169)
9. Advisory board for state cooperatives (Section 1322(b)(3), p. 173)
10. Private purchasing council for state cooperatives (Section 1322(d), p. 177)
11. State basic health plan programs (Section 1331, p. 201)
12. State-based reinsurance program (Section 1341, p. 226)
13. Program of risk corridors for individual and small group markets (Section 1342, p. 233)
14. Program to determine eligibility for Exchange participation (Section 1411, p. 267)
15. Program for advance determination of tax credit eligibility (Section 1412, p. 288)
16. Grant program to implement health IT enrollment standards

(Section 1561, p. 370)
17. Federal Coordinated Health Care Office for dual eligible beneficiaries (Section 2602, p. 512)
18. Medicaid quality measurement program (Section 2701, p. 518)
19. Medicaid health home program for people with chronic conditions, and grants for planning same (Section 2703, p. 524)
20. Medicaid demonstration project to evaluate bundled payments (Section 2704, p. 532)
21. Medicaid demonstration project for global payment system (Section 2705, p. 536)
22. Medicaid demonstration project for accountable care organizations (Section 2706, p. 538)
23. Medicaid demonstration project for emergency psychiatric care (Section 2707, p. 540)
24. Grant program for delivery of services to individuals with postpartum depression (Section 2952(b), p. 591)
25. State allotments for grants to promote personal responsibility education programs (Section 2953, p. 596)
26. Medicare value-based purchasing program (Section 3001(a), p. 613)
27. Medicare value-based purchasing demonstration program for critical access hospitals (Section 3001(b), p. 637)
28. Medicare value-based purchasing program for skilled nursing facilities (Section 3006(a), p. 666)
29. Medicare value-based purchasing program for home health agencies (Section 3006(b), p. 668)
30. Interagency Working Group on Health Care Quality (Section 3012, p. 688)
31. Grant program to develop health care quality measures (Section 3013, p. 693)
32. Center for Medicare and Medicaid Innovation (Section 3021, p. 712)
33. Medicare shared savings program (Section 3022, p. 728)
34. Medicare pilot program on payment bundling (Section 3023, p. 739)
35. Independence at home medical practice demonstration program (Section 3024, p. 752)
36. Program for use of patient safety organizations to reduce hospital readmission rates (Section 3025(b), p. 775)

37. Community-based care transitions program (Section 3026, p. 776)
38. Demonstration project for payment of complex diagnostic laboratory tests (Section 3113, p. 800)
39. Medicare hospice concurrent care demonstration project (Section 3140, p. 850)
40. Independent Payment Advisory Board (Section 3403, p. 982)
41. Consumer Advisory Council for Independent Payment Advisory Board (Section 3403, p. 1027)
42. Grant program for technical assistance to providers implementing health quality practices (Section 3501, p. 1043)
43. Grant program to establish interdisciplinary health teams (Section 3502, p. 1048)
44. Grant program to implement medication therapy management (Section 3503, p. 1055)
45. Grant program to support emergency care pilot programs (Section 3504, p. 1061)
46. Grant program to promote universal access to trauma services (Section 3505(b), p. 1081)
47. Grant program to develop and promote shared decision-making aids (Section 3506, p. 1088)
48. Grant program to support implementation of shared decision-making (Section 3506, p. 1091)
49. Grant program to integrate quality improvement in clinical education (Section 3508, p. 1095)
50. Health and Human Services Coordinating Committee on Women's Health (Section 3509(a), p. 1098)
51. Centers for Disease Control Office of Women's Health (Section 3509(b), p. 1102)
52. Agency for Health care Research and Quality Office of Women's Health (Section 3509(e), p. 1105)
53. Health Resources and Services Administration Office of Women's Health (Section 3509(f), p. 1106)
54. Food and Drug Administration Office of Women's Health (Section 3509(g), p. 1109)
55. National Prevention, Health Promotion, and Public Health Council (Section 4001, p. 1114)
56. Advisory Group on Prevention, Health Promotion, and Integrative and Public Health (Section 4001(f), p. 1117)

57. Prevention and Public Health Fund (Section 4002, p. 1121)
58. Community Preventive Services Task Force (Section 4003(b), p. 1126)
59. Grant program to support school-based health centers (Section 4101, p. 1135)
60. Grant program to promote research-based dental caries disease management (Section 4102, p. 1147)
61. Grant program for States to prevent chronic disease in Medicaid beneficiaries (Section 4108, p. 1174)
62. Community transformation grants (Section 4201, p. 1182)
63. Grant program to provide public health interventions (Section 4202, p. 1188)
64. Demonstration program of grants to improve child immunization rates (Section 4204(b), p. 1200)
65. Pilot program for risk-factor assessments provided through community health centers (Section 4206, p. 1215)
66. Grant program to increase epidemiology and laboratory capacity (Section 4304, p. 1233)
67. Interagency Pain Research Coordinating Committee (Section 4305, p. 1238)
68. National Health Care Workforce Commission (Section 5101, p. 1256)
69. Grant program to plan health care workforce development activities (Section 5102(c), p. 1275)
70. Grant program to implement health care workforce development activities (Section 5102(d), p. 1279)
71. Pediatric specialty loan repayment program (Section 5203, p. 1295)
72. Public Health Workforce Loan Repayment Program (Section 5204, p. 1300)
73. Allied Health Loan Forgiveness Program (Section 5205, p. 1305)
74. Grant program to provide mid-career training for health professionals (Section 5206, p. 1307)
75. Grant program to fund nurse-managed health clinics (Section 5208, p. 1310)
76. Grant program to support primary care training programs (Section 5301, p. 1315)
77. Grant program to fund training for direct care workers (Section 5302, p. 1322)

78. Grant program to develop dental training programs (Section 5303, p. 1325)
79. Demonstration program to increase access to dental health care in underserved communities (Section 5304, p. 1331)
80. Grant program to promote geriatric education centers (Section 5305, p. 1334)
81. Grant program to promote health professionals entering geriatrics (Section 5305, p. 1339)
82. Grant program to promote training in mental and behavioral health (Section 5306, p. 1344)
83. Grant program to promote nurse retention programs (Section 5309, p. 1354)
84. Student loan forgiveness for nursing school faculty (Section 5311(b), p. 1360)
85. Grant program to promote positive health behaviors and outcomes (Section 5313, p. 1364)
86. Public Health Sciences Track for medical students (Section 5315, p. 1372)
87. Primary Care Extension Program to educate providers (Section 5405, p. 1404)
88. Grant program for demonstration projects to address health workforce shortage needs (Section 5507, p. 1442)
89. Grant program for demonstration projects to develop training programs for home health aides (Section 5507, p. 1447)
90. Grant program to establish new primary care residency programs (Section 5508(a), p. 1458)
91. Program of payments to teaching health centers that sponsor medical residency training (Section 5508(c), p. 1462)
92. Graduate nurse education demonstration program (Section 5509, p. 1472)
93. Grant program to establish demonstration projects for community-based mental health settings (Section 5604, p. 1486)
94. Commission on Key National Indicators (Section 5605, p. 1489)
95. Quality assurance and performance improvement program for skilled nursing facilities (Section 6102, p. 1554)
96. Special focus facility program for skilled nursing facilities (Section 6103(a)(3), p. 1561)
97. Special focus facility program for nursing facilities (Section 6103(b)(3), p. 1568)

98. National independent monitor pilot program for skilled nursing facilities and nursing facilities (Section 6112, p. 1589)
99. Demonstration projects for nursing facilities involved in the culture change movement (Section 6114, p. 1597)
100. Patient-Centered Outcomes Research Institute (Section 6301, p. 1619)
101. Standing methodology committee for Patient-Centered Outcomes Research Institute (Section 6301, p. 1629)
102. Board of Governors for Patient-Centered Outcomes Research Institute (Section 6301, p. 1638)
103. Patient-Centered Outcomes Research Trust Fund (Section 6301(e), p. 1656)
104. Elder Justice Coordinating Council (Section 6703, p. 1773)
105. Advisory Board on Elder Abuse, Neglect, and Exploitation (Section 6703, p. 1776)
106. Grant program to create elder abuse forensic centers (Section 6703, p. 1783)
107. Grant program to promote continuing education for long-term care staffers (Section 6703, p. 1787)
108. Grant program to improve management practices and training (Section 6703, p. 1788)
109. Grant program to subsidize costs of electronic health records (Section 6703, p. 1791)
110. Grant program to promote adult protective services (Section 6703, p. 1796)
111. Grant program to conduct elder abuse detection and prevention (Section 6703, p. 1798)
112. Grant program to support long-term care ombudsmen (Section 6703, p. 1800)
113. National Training Institute for long-term care surveyors (Section 6703, p. 1806)
114. Grant program to fund State surveys of long-term care residences (Section 6703, p. 1809)
115. CLASS Independence Fund (Section 8002, p. 1926)
116. CLASS Independence Fund Board of Trustees (Section 8002, p. 1927)
117. CLASS Independence Advisory Council (Section 8002, p. 1931)
118. Personal Care Attendants Workforce Advisory Panel (Section 8002(c), p. 1938)

119. Multi-state health plans offered by Office of Personnel Management (Section 10104(p), p. 2086)
120. Advisory board for multi-state health plans (Section 10104(p), p. 2094)
121. Pregnancy Assistance Fund (Section 10212, p. 2164)
122. Value-based purchasing program for ambulatory surgical centers (Section 10301, p. 2176)
123. Demonstration project for payment adjustments to home health services (Section 10315, p. 2200)
124. Pilot program for care of individuals in environmental emergency declaration areas (Section 10323, p. 2223)
125. Grant program to screen at-risk individuals for environmental health conditions (Section 10323(b), p. 2231)
126. Pilot programs to implement value-based purchasing (Section 10326, p. 2242)
127. Grant program to support community-based collaborative care networks (Section 10333, p. 2265)
128. Centers for Disease Control Office of Minority Health (Section 10334, p. 2272)
129. Health Resources and Services Administration Office of Minority Health (Section 10334, p. 2272)
130. Substance Abuse and Mental Health Services Administration Office of Minority Health (Section 10334, p. 2272)
131. Agency for Health care Research and Quality Office of Minority Health (Section 10334, p. 2272)
132. Food and Drug Administration Office of Minority Health (Section 10334, p. 2272)
133. Centers for Medicare and Medicaid Services Office of Minority Health (Section 10334, p. 2272)
134. Grant program to promote small business wellness programs (Section 10408, p. 2285)
135. Cures Acceleration Network (Section 10409, p. 2289)
136. Cures Acceleration Network Review Board (Section 10409, p. 2291)
137. Grant program for Cures Acceleration Network (Section 10409, p. 2297)
138. Grant program to promote centers of excellence for depression (Section 10410, p. 2304)
139. Advisory committee for young women's breast health awareness education campaign (Section 10413, p. 2322)

140. Grant program to provide assistance to provide information to young women with breast cancer (Section 10413, p. 2326)
141. Interagency Access to Health Care in Alaska Task Force (Section 10501, p. 2329)
142. Grant program to train nurse practitioners as primary care providers (Section 10501(e), p. 2332)
143. Grant program for community-based diabetes prevention (Section 10501(g), p. 2337)
144. Grant program for providers who treat a high percentage of medically underserved populations (Section 10501(k), p. 2343)
145. Grant program to recruit students to practice in underserved communities (Section 10501(l), p. 2344)
146. Community Health Center Fund (Section 10503, p. 2355)
147. Demonstration project to provide access to health care for the uninsured at reduced fees (Section 10504, p. 2357)
148. Demonstration program to explore alternatives to tort litigation (Section 10607, p. 2369)
149. Indian Health demonstration program for chronic shortages of health professionals (S. 1790, Section 112, p. 24)*
150. Office of Indian Men's Health (S. 1790, Section 136, p. 71)*
151. Indian Country modular component facilities demonstration program (S. 1790, Section 146, p. 108)*
152. Indian mobile health stations demonstration program (S. 1790, Section 147, p. 111)*
153. Office of Direct Service Tribes (S. 1790, Section 172, p. 151)*
154. Indian Health Service mental health technician training program (S. 1790, Section 181, p. 173)*
155. Indian Health Service program for treatment of child sexual abuse victims (S. 1790, Section 181, p. 192)*
156. Indian Health Service program for treatment of domestic violence and sexual abuse (S. 1790, Section 181, p. 194)*
157. Indian youth telemental health demonstration project (S. 1790, Section 181, p. 204)*
158. Indian youth life skills demonstration project (S. 1790, Section 181, p. 220)*
159. Indian Health Service Director of HIV/AIDS Prevention and Treatment (S. 1790, Section 199B, p. 258)*

*Section 10221, page 2173 of H.R. 3590 deems that S. 1790 shall be deemed as passed with certain amendments.

SEC. 2793. HEALTH INSURANCE CONSUMER INFORMATIO N	(d) DATA COLLECTIO N.	$30,000,000	2) AUTHORIZATION FOR SUBSEQUENT YEARS.—There is authorized to be appropriated to the Secretary for each fiscal year following the fiscal year described in paragraph (1), such sums as may be necessary to carry out this section.
SEC. 2794. ENSURING THAT CONSUMERS GET VALUE FOR THEIR DOLLARS.	(1) PREMIUM REVIEW GRANTS DURING 2010 THROUGH 2014.	$250,000,000	INITIAL PREMIUM REVIEW PROCESS.
SEC. 1101. IMMEDIATE ACCESS TO INSURANCE FOR UNINSURED INDIVIDUALS WITH A PREEXISTING CONDITION.		$5,000,000,000	
SEC. 1102. REINSURANC E FOR EARLY RETIREES.		$5,000,000,000	

SEC. 1322. FEDERAL PROGRAM TO ASSIST ESTABLISHMENT AND OPERATION OF NONPROFIT, MEMBER-RUN HEALTH INSURANCE ISSUERS.		$6,000,000,000	
SEC. 2405. FUNDING TO EXPAND STATE AGING AND DISABILITY RESOURCE CENTERS.		$50,000,000	
SEC. 1139B. ADULT HEALTH QUALITY MEASURES.	(5) ESTABLISHMENT OF MEDICAID QUALITY MEASUREMENT PROGRAM.	$300,000,000	'(a) DEVELOPMENT OF CORE SET OF HEALTH CARE QUALITY MEASURES FOR ADULTS ELIGIBLE FOR BENEFITS UNDER MEDICAID.
SEC. 2707. MEDICAID EMERGENCY PSYCHIATRIC DEMONSTRATION PROJECT.		$75,000,000	
SEC. 2801. MACPAC ASSESSMENT OF POLICIES AFFECTING		$9,000,000	Subtitle J—Improvements to the Medicaid and CHIP Payment and Access Commission

ALL MEDICAID BENEFICIARIES.			(MACPAC)
SEC. 2951. MATERNAL, INFANT, AND EARLY CHILDHOOD HOME VISITING PROGRAMS.		$1,500,000,000	'(b) REQUIREMENT FOR ALL STATES TO ASSESS STATEWIDE NEEDS AND IDENTIFY AT RISK COMMUNITIES. '(4) PRIORITY FOR SERVING HIGH-RISK POPULATIONS.
SEC. 512. SERVICES TO INDIVIDUALS WITH A POSTPARTUM CONDITION AND THEIR FAMILIES.		$3,000,000	(B) such sums as may be necessary for fiscal years 2011 and 2012.
SEC. 513. PERSONAL RESPONSIBILITY EDUCATION.	(1) GRANTS TO IMPLEMENT INNOVATIVE STRATEGIES.	$10,000,000	Politically correct for sex education, relationships, growing up things like we learned in home economics
SEC. 513. PERSONAL RESPONSIBILITY EDUCATION.	(6) DATA COLLECTION AND REPORTING.	$375,000,000	

SEC. 3014. QUALITY MEASUREMENT.	(b) PROCESS FOR DISSEMINATION OF MEASURES USED BY THE SECRETARY.	$100,000,000	A quality control group of stakeholders? (a) NEW DUTIES FOR CONSENSUS-BASED ENTITY.— (1) MULTI-STAKEHOLDER GROUP INPUT.—Section 1890(b) of the Social Security Act (42 U.S.C. 1395aaa(b)), as amended by section 3003, is amended by adding at the end the following new paragraphs: ''(7) CONVENING MULTI-STAKEHOLDER GROUPS.
SEC. 3021. ESTABLISHMENT OF CENTER FOR MEDICARE AND MEDICAID INNOVATION WITHIN CMS.		$5,000,000	design, implementation, and evaluation of models under subsection (b) for fiscal year 2010
SEC. 3021. ESTABLISHMENT OF CENTER FOR MEDICARE AND MEDICAID INNOVATION WITHIN CMS.		$10,000,000,000	2011-2019

SEC. 3024. INDEPENDENCE AT HOME DEMONSTRATION PROGRAM.		$30,000,000	2010-2015 Centers for Medicare & Medicaid Services Program Management Account
SEC. 3113. TREATMENT OF CERTAIN COMPLEX DIAGNOSTIC LABORATORY TESTS.		$5,000,000	
SEC. 3201. MEDICARE ADVANTAGE PAYMENT.		$5,000,000,000	Transition payments
SEC. 3306. FUNDING OUTREACH AND ASSISTANCE FOR LOW-INCOME PROGRAMS.	State insurance funding	$22,500,000	
SEC. 3306. FUNDING OUTREACH AND ASSISTANCE FOR LOW-INCOME PROGRAMS.	Agencies on aging	$22,500,000	
SEC. 3306. FUNDING OUTREACH AND ASSISTANCE FOR LOW-INCOME PROGRAMS.	Aging and disability	$15,000,000	

SEC. 3306. FUNDING OUTREACH AND ASSISTANCE FOR LOW-INCOME PROGRAMS.	(d) ADDITIONAL FUNDING FOR CONTRACT WITH THE ENTER FOR BENEFITS AND OUTREACH ENROLLMENT	$10,000,000	
SEC. 3403. INDEPENDENT MEDICARE ADVISORY BOARD.	(4) MEDICARE PROGRAM SPENDING.	$75,000,000	2012-2016 with additional - each year gets $15,000,000 + CPI raise/Board of 15 unelected people
SEC. 933. HEALTH CARE DELIVERY SYSTEM RESEARCH.		$100,000,000	2010-2014
SEC. 1204. COMPETITIVE GRANTS FOR REGIONALIZED SYSTEMS FOR EMERGENCY CARE RESPONSE.		$120,000,000	2010-2014 States need matching funds agreements
SEC. 3505. TRAUMA CARE CENTERS AND SERVICE AVAILABILITY.	SEC. 1245. AUTHORIZATION OF APPROPRIATIONS.	$100,000,000	Emergency and Uncompensated care costs

PART H—TRAUMA SERVICE AVAILABILITY	SEC. 1282. AUTHORIZATION OF APPROPRIATIONS.	$600,000,000	2010-2015 SEC. 1281. GRANTS TO STATES.
SEC. 3510. PATIENT NAVIGATOR PROGRAM.	Women's health programs	$3,500,000	and such sums as may be necessary for each of fiscal years 2011 through 2015.
SEC. 4002. PREVENTION AND PUBLIC HEALTH FUND.		$7,000,000,000	2010-2015 $2,000,000,000 per year after that. To provide for expanded and sustained national investment in prevention and public health programs to improve health and help restrain the rate of growth in private and public sector health care costs.
SEC. 4004. EDUCATION AND OUTREACH CAMPAIGN REGARDING PREVENTIVE BENEFITS.		$500,000,000	shall be expended on the campaigns and activities required under this section
Subtitle B—Increasing Access to Clinical Preventive Services	SEC. 4101. SCHOOL-BASED HEALTH CENTERS.	$200,000,000	2010-2013 School-Based Health Center
SEC. 4108. INCENTIVES FOR PREVENTION		$100,000,000	

OF CHRONIC DISEASES IN MEDICAID.			
SEC. 4202. HEALTHY AGING, LIVING WELL; EVALUATION OF COMMUNITY-BASED PREVENTION AND WELLNESS PROGRAMS FOR MEDICARE BENEFICIARIES.		$50,000,000	
SEC. 4204. IMMUNIZATIONS.		$1,000,000	
SEC. 2821. EPIDEMIOLOGY-LABORATORY CAPACITY GRANTS.	Subtitle C—Strengthening Public Health Surveillance Systems	$1,140,000,000	
SEC. 4306. FUNDING FOR CHILDHOOD OBESITY DEMONSTRATION PROJECT.		$25,000,000	

SEC. 5102. STATE HEALTH CARE WORKFORCE DEVELOPME NT GRANTS.	Planning grants	$8,000,000	and such sums as may be necessary for each subsequent fiscal year.
SEC. 5102. STATE HEALTH CARE WORKFORCE DEVELOPME NT GRANTS.	Implement ation grants	$150,000,000	and such sums as may be necessary for each subsequent fiscal year. States must match what they receive
SEC. 5103. HEALTH CARE WORKFORCE ASSESSMENT .	(A) NATIONAL CENTER.	$37,500,000	2010-2014 (c) STATE AND REGIONAL CENTERS FOR HEALTH WORKFORCE ANALYSIS.
SEC. 5103. HEALTH CARE WORKFORCE ASSESSMENT .	(B) STATE AND REGIONAL CENTERS.	$22,500,000	2010-2014 (c) STATE AND REGIONAL CENTERS FOR HEALTH WORKFORCE ANALYSIS.
SEC. 775. INVESTMENT IN TOMORROW 'S PEDIATRIC HEALTH CARE WORKFORCE .		$30,000,000	
SEC. 775. INVESTMENT IN TOMORROW 'S PEDIATRIC HEALTH		$80,000,000	2010-2013

CARE WORKFORCE.			
SEC. 776. PUBLIC HEALTH WORKFORCE LOAN REPAYMENT PROGRAM.		$195,000,000	and such sums as may be necessary for each of fiscal years 2011 through 2015
SEC. 777. TRAINING FOR MID-CAREER PUBLIC AND ALLIED HEALTH PROFESSIONALS.		$60,000,000	and such sums as may be necessary for each of fiscal years 2011 through 2015
SEC. 5207. FUNDING FOR NATIONAL HEALTH SERVICE CORPS.		$4,009,000,000	2010-2015 and each subsequent fiscal year + increase formula
SEC. 330A–1. GRANTS TO NURSE–MANAGED HEALTH CLINICS.		$50,000,000	and such sums as may be necessary for each of fiscal years 2011 through 2014
SEC. 203. COMMISSIONED CORPS AND READY RESERVE CORPS.		$25,000,000	National emergency corp - not the military reserve?

SEC. 203. COMMISSIONED CORPS AND READY RESERVE CORPS.		$12,500,000	Ready reserve corps 2010-2014
SEC. 747. PRIMARY CARE TRAINING AND ENHANCEMENT.		$125,000,000	and such sums as may be necessary for each of fiscal years 2011 through 2014
SEC. 747. PRIMARY CARE TRAINING AND ENHANCEMENT.	(3) INTEGRATING ACADEMIC ADMINISTRATIVE UNITS.	$3,750,000	2010-2014
SEC. 747A. TRAINING OPPORTUNITIES FOR DIRECT CARE WORKERS.		$10,000,000	2011-2013
SEC. 748. TRAINING IN GENERAL, PEDIATRIC, AND PUBLIC HEALTH DENTISTRY.		$30,000,000	and such sums as may be necessary for each of fiscal years 2011 through 2015
SEC. 5304. ALTERNATIVE DENTAL HEALTH CARE PROVIDERS DEMONSTRATION		$4,000,000	not less than this amount. Applies to underserved communities

PROJECT.			
SEC. 5305. GERIATRIC EDUCATION AND TRAINING; CAREER AWARDS; COMPREHEN SIVE GERIATRIC EDUCATION.		$10,800,000	2011-2014
SEC. 5305. GERIATRIC EDUCATION AND TRAINING; CAREER AWARDS; COMPREHEN SIVE GERIATRIC EDUCATION.		$10,000,000	2011-2013
SEC. 756. MENTAL AND BEHAVIORAL HEALTH EDUCATION AND TRAINING GRANTS.		$8,000,000	2010-2013 Social work training
SEC. 756. MENTAL AND BEHAVIORAL HEALTH EDUCATION		$12,000,000	2010-2013 Gradiate psychology

AND TRAINING GRANTS.			
SEC. 756. MENTAL AND BEHAVIORAL HEALTH EDUCATION AND TRAINING GRANTS.		$10,000,000	2010-2013 child and adolescent mental health
SEC. 756. MENTAL AND BEHAVIORAL HEALTH EDUCATION AND TRAINING GRANTS.		$5,000,000	2010-2013
SEC. 847. ELIGIBLE INDIVIDUAL STUDENT LOAN REPAYMENT.		$338,000,000	and such sums as may be necessary for each of fiscal years 2011 through 2016
SEC. 778. FELLOWSHIP TRAINING IN APPLIED PUBLIC HEALTH EPIDEMIOLO GY, PUBLIC HEALTH LABORATORY SCIENCE, PUBLIC HEALTH INFORMATIC		$79,000,000	2010-2013

S, AND EXPANSION OF THE EPIDEMIC INTELLIGENCE SERVICE.			
SEC. 5401. CENTERS OF EXCELLENCE.	Subtitle E—Supporting the Existing Health Care Workforce	$50,000,000	2010-2015 and such sums as may be necessary for each subsequent fiscal year. To colleges - what agenda do you think their going to support?
SEC. 5402. HEALTH CARE PROFESSIONALS TRAINING FOR DIVERSITY.	Scholarships for disadvantaged students	$51,000,000	2010 and such sums as may be necessary for each of the fiscal years 2011 through 2014
SEC. 751. AREA HEALTH EDUCATION CENTERS.		$62,500,000	2010-2014 Colleges
SEC. 752. CONTINUING EDUCATIONAL SUPPORT FOR HEALTH PROFESSIONALS SERVING IN UNDERSERVE		$25,000,000	2010-2014 and such sums as may be necessary for each subsequent fiscal year. Tied to underserved communities

D COMMUNITIES.			
SEC. 5405. PRIMARY CARE EXTENSION PROGRAM.	SEC. 399W. PRIMARY CARE EXTENSION PROGRAM.	$240,000,000	2011-2012 and such sums as may be necessary for each of fiscal years 2013 through 2014
SEC. 5507. DEMONSTRATION PROJECTS TO ADDRESS HEALTH PROFESSIONS WORKFORCE NEEDS; EXTENSION OF FAMILY-TO-FAMILY HEALTH INFORMATION CENTERS.	SEC. 2008. DEMONSTRATION PROJECTS TO ADDRESS HEALTH PROFESSIONS WORKFORCE NEEDS.	$425,000,000	2010-2014
SEC. 749A. TEACHING HEALTH CENTERS DEVELOPMENT GRANTS.		$125,000,000	2010-2012
SEC. 340H. PROGRAM OF PAYMENTS TO TEACHING HEALTH		$230,000,000	2011-2015

CENTERS THAT OPERATE GRADUATE MEDICAL EDUCATION PROGRAMS.			
SEC. 5509. GRADUATE NURSE EDUCATION DEMONSTRATION.		$200,000,000	2012-2015
SEC. 5601. SPENDING FOR FEDERALLY QUALIFIED HEALTH CENTERS (FQHCS).	Subtitle G—Improving Access to Health Care Services	$33,956,000,000	2010-2015 2016 and each subsequent fiscal year +increase formula
SEC. 5603. REAUTHORIZATION OF THE WAKEFIELD EMERGENCY MEDICAL SERVICES FOR CHILDREN PROGRAM.		$138,390,781	2010-2013
SEC. 520K. AWARDS FOR CO-LOCATING PRIMARY AND SPECIALTY CARE IN COMMUNITY		$50,000,000	and such sums as may be necessary for each of fiscal years 2011 through 2014

-BASED MENTAL HEALTH SETTINGS.			
SEC. 5605. KEY NATIONAL INDICATORS.	(d) GOVERNMENT ACCOUNTABILITY OFFICE STUDY AND REPORT	$10,000,000	2010-2018
SEC. 9511. PATIENT-CENTERED OUTCOMES RESEARCH TRUST FUND.		$1,260,000,000	2010-2019
SEC. 9511. PATIENT-CENTERED OUTCOMES RESEARCH TRUST FUND.		$100,000,000	2011-2020
SEC. 2022. ADVISORY BOARD ON ELDER ABUSE, NEGLECT, AND EXPLOITATION.	SEC. 2024. AUTHORIZATION OF APPROPRIATIONS.	$27,500,000	2011-2014

SEC. 2031. ESTABLISHMENT AND SUPPORT OF ELDER ABUSE, NEGLECT, AND EXPLOITATION FORENSIC CENTERS.		$26,000,000	2011-2014
SEC. 2041. ENHANCEMENT OF LONG-TERM CARE.	PART II—PROGRAMS TO PROMOTE ELDER JUSTICE	$67,000,000	2011-2014
SEC. 2042. ADULT PROTECTIVE SERVICES FUNCTIONS AND GRANT PROGRAMS.		$15,000,000	2011-2014
SEC. 2042. ADULT PROTECTIVE SERVICES FUNCTIONS AND GRANT PROGRAMS.		$500,000,000	2011-2014
SEC. 2042. ADULT PROTECTIVE SERVICES FUNCTIONS AND GRANT PROGRAMS.		$100,000,000	2011-2014

SEC. 2043. LONG-TERM CARE OMBUDSMAN PROGRAM GRANTS AND TRAINING.		$37,500,000	2011-2014
SEC. 2043. LONG-TERM CARE OMBUDSMAN PROGRAM GRANTS AND TRAINING.		$40,000,000	2011-2014
SEC. 2044. PROVISION OF INFORMATION REGARDING, AND EVALUATIONS OF, ELDER JUSTICE PROGRAMS.		$12,000,000	2011-2014
SEC. 2044. PROVISION OF INFORMATION REGARDING, AND EVALUATIONS OF, ELDER JUSTICE PROGRAMS.		$20,000,000	2011-2014
SEC. 10212. ESTABLISHMENT OF PREGNANCY ASSISTANCE		$250,000,000	2010-2019 Matching requirement grant

FUND.			
SEC. 2009. PROGRAM FOR EARLY DETECTION OF CERTAIN MEDICAL CONDITIONS RELATED TO ENVIRONME NTAL HEALTH HAZARDS.		$23,000,000	2010-2014 $20M for each 5 year period thereafter
SEC. 10408. GRANTS FOR SMALL BUSINESSES TO PROVIDE COMPREHEN SIVE WORKPLACE WELLNESS PROGRAMS.		$200,000,000	2011-2015
SEC. 402C. CURES ACCELERATI ON NETWORK.		$500,000,000	2010 and such sums as may be necessary for subsequent fiscal years.
SEC. 520B. NATIONAL CENTERS OF EXCELLENCE FOR DEPRESSION.		$500,000,000	2011-2015
SEC. 520B. NATIONAL CENTERS OF		$750,000,000	2016-2020

EXCELLENCE FOR DEPRESSION.			
SEC. 399NN. YOUNG WOMEN'S BREAST HEALTH AWARENESS AND SUPPORT OF YOUNG WOMEN DIAGNOSED WITH BREAST CANCER.		$45,000,000	2010-2014
SEC. 749B. RURAL PHYSICIAN TRAINING GRANTS.		$4,000,000	2010-2013
SEC. 768. PREVENTIVE MEDICINE AND PUBLIC HEALTH TRAINING GRANT PROGRAM.		$43,000,000	2011 and such sums as may be necessary for each of the fiscal years 2012 through 2015
SEC. 10502. INFRASTRUCTURE TO EXPAND ACCESS TO CARE.		$100,000,000	2010
SEC. 10503. COMMUNITY HEALTH CENTERS AND THE		$49,000,000,000	2011-2015

NATIONAL HEALTH SERVICE CORPS FUND.			
SEC. 399V–4. STATE DEMONSTRATION PROGRAMS TO EVALUATE ALTERNATIVES TO CURRENT MEDICAL TORT LITIGATION.		$50,000,000	2011-2015
TOTAL	**$138,384,440,781**		

APPENDIX D – Early Retiree Reinsurance Plan

List of those receiving money came from the following websites:

http://www.buckconsultants.com/portals/0/publications/fyi/2012/fyi-2012-0224-Early-Retiree-Rein-Prgm-Funds-Exhausted.pdf
and more can be found at:

http://www.health care.gov/law/features/employers/early-retiree-reinsurance-plan/mi.html

Compilation of entities that received money under this program:

Commercial Organizations (834) received $1,779,774,095 - 37.8%

Governmental Entities (1,326) received $2,100,337,403 - 44.6%

Unions (495) received $781,209,744 - 16.6%

Nonprofit Organizations (139) received $40,006,145 - 0.8%

Others (5) received $12,940,130 - 0.3%

Total $4,714,267,517

Recipients and amount received:

State of New Jersey Treasury Department $98,606,767

Commonwealth of Kentucky $95,474,718

State of New York $88,424,151

Board of Trustees of North Carolina Teachers' and State Employees' Comprehensive Major Medical Plan $87,462,204

State Teachers Retirement System of Ohio $78,693,323

State of Michigan Public School Employees Retirement System $64,379,629

National Carriers' Conference Committee $60,016,187

Georgia Department of Community Health $57,936,127

Commonwealth of Massachusetts $51,311,601

The Boeing Company $50,160,905

State of Michigan $46,936,210

Alcatel-Lucent USA Inc. $42,438,274

United Parcel Service of America, Inc. $37,394,549

Commonwealth of Pennsylvania $32,192,146

Public Education Employees Health Insurance Fund—Alabama $32,040,120

Employees Retirement System of Texas (ERS) $30,175,627

State of Alaska Retirement and Benefits Plans $27,637,600 0.6%

South Carolina Budget & Control Board, Employee Insurance Program $27,142,502

Arizona State Retirement System $19,977,697

Department of Finance and Administration—Mississippi $19,890,691

Oregon Educators Benefit Board $19,446,347

The Boeing Company $50,160,905

Alcatel-Lucent USA Inc. $42,438,274

General Motors LLC $31,282,424

International Business Machines Corporation (IBM) $30,963,516

Deere & Company $28,083,767

Delta Air Lines, Inc. $27,309,420

American Airlines Inc. $24,260,058

Qwest Communications International Inc. $23,584,496

Pfizer Inc. $23,001,263

Caterpillar Inc. $20,335,732

The Procter & Gamble Company $19,186,151

Alcoa Inc. $17,404,025

Ford Motor Company $17,290,036

The Dow Chemical Company $16,255,671

BP Corporation North America Inc. $16,179,320

E.I. DuPont de Nemours and Company $15,401,279

National Carriers' Conference Committee $60,016,187

Wisconsin Education Association Insurance Trust $33,459,558

SISC III Health & Welfare $27,492,509

Trustees of the Central States, SE & SW Areas H&W Fund—Illinois $22,716,745

Joint Plan Committee—Delaware $14,803,314 0.3%

Steelworkers Health and Welfare Fund $12,503,419

Maine Education Association Benefits Trust $8,862,203

UFCW & Employers Benefit Trust $8,825,664

Boilermakers National Health and Welfare Fund $7,668,334

National Automatic Sprinkler Industry Welfare Fund Joint Board of Trustees $6,956,390

Michigan Conference of Teamsters Welfare Fund $6,040,715

Chicago District Council of Carpenters Welfare Fund $5,164,412

Pension, Hospitalization and Benefit Plan of the Electrical Industry $4,920,494

Governing Committee—Delaware $4,600,801

1199 SEIU National Benefit Fund for Health and Human Service Employees $4,359,989

Management–Ila Managed Health Care Trust Fund $4,291,264

Insurance and Benefits Trust of Peace Officers Research Association of California $3,207,969

Screen Actors Guild–Producers Health Plan $3,049,896

Midwest Operating Engineers Welfare Fund $2,999,218

Nonprofit recipients:

Blue Cross Blue Shield of Michigan $3,713,920

Kaiser Foundation Health Plan, Inc. $948,844

President and Fellows of Harvard College $929,113

Independence Blue Cross $746,570

Yale University $713,799

Trustees of Princeton University $706,165

Duke University $604,797

Chandler Health Care Benefits Trust $574,218

Eastern Maine Health care Systems $484,937

Massachusetts Institute of Technology $481,345

Cornell University $472,607

Community Hospital of the Monterey Peninsula $463,760

New York University $454,544

Read more at http://freedomoutpost.com/2013/10/obamacare-appropriations-billions-taxpayer-dollars-werent-told-even-passed-law/#k2JeKF6XFxlEOMsU.99

References

[1] Lamb: Obama Transforming America By Henry Lamb April 4, 2011 6:22 am <http://www.gopusa.com/commentary/2011/04/04/obama-transforming-america/>
[2] ObamaCare Survival Guide by Nicholas J. Tate location 444
[3] From <http://townhall.com/tipsheet/sarahjeanseman/2014/02/07/poll-obamacare-just-as-baffling-to-americans-now-as-in-september-n1791338?utm_source=thdailypm&utm_medium=email&utm_campaign=nl_pm
[4]ObamaCare Survival Guide by Nicholas J. Tate "But as bold and sweeping as that action is, it still would leave more than 20 million Americans without health insurance in 2019." location 1316
[5] While the numbers change depending on the year and the source, you can reliably say that a small percentage of actual uninsured is not a credible justification to pass such a large bill that affects our health care and GDP like HR 3590 does. "Uninsured: According to the 2010 U.S. Census, 49.9 million people say they are uninsured. But 14 million of them are already eligible for government programs such as Medicaid or CHIP (for children) and haven't signed up. Another 7.6 million have household incomes over $75,000. That leaves about 28.3 million people who probably cannot afford insurance. About 18 million of them are American citizens. *Decoding the Obama Health Law: What you Need to know - Betsy McCaughey - read more at location 1514*" Or see, "In 2000 about 38 million Americans were uninsured. With the recent economic downturn that number had spiked to 50 million by 2010—a 32 percent increase compared to a decade ago. *ObamaCare Survival Guide by Nicholas J. Tate Read more at location 862*"
[6] HR 3950, Section 10106(a)(2)(A), pg 789.
[7] *The Scheme behind the Obamacare Fraud*, Andrew C. McCarthy, 11/23/13, National Review Online, http://www.nationalreview.com/article/364667/scheme-behind-obamacare-fraud-andrew-c-mccarthy
[8] *Id.*
[9] Decoding the Obama Health Law: What you Need to know - Betsy McCaughey Read more at location 1044
[10] Constitutional Interpretation, https://www.thefederalistpapers.org/principles-of-constitutional-interpretation
[11] *Head Money Cases*, 112 U.S. 580 (1884).
[12] <http://www.gopusa.com/commentary/2011/11/30/landrith-supreme-court-impartiality-and-obamacare/?subscriber=1> Landrith: Supreme Court Impartiality and ObamaCare, By George Landrith November 30, 2011 7:22 am
It is becoming more and more difficult to argue that Elena Kagan didn't in her capacity as a high ranking government lawyer participate as counsel or adviser concerning the constitutionality of ObamaCare. It is also appears increasingly unlikely that she did not express an opinion concerning the constitutionality of the law. And the Obama Administration's reluctance to provide a full accounting of the relevant communications is particularly troubling. This does not pass the sniff test.

> Now let's turn to the claims that Associate Justice Elena Kagan should recuse herself. The real issue boils down to did she "serve in governmental employment and in such capacity participated as counsel [or] adviser ... concerning the proceeding or expressed an opinion concerning the merits of the particular case in controversy?"
>
> Before President Obama appointed Ms. Kagan to the Supreme Court, she worked at the Department of Justice as the Administration's Solicitor General, the government's top lawyer before the Supreme Court. If Kagan were still working at the Justice Department, she would be the lawyer arguing that ObamaCare is

constitutional, rather than a judge hearing and deciding the case.

During her confirmation hearing, Kagan was asked if she had offered or been asked her opinion on the health care law or its underlying constitutionality. She answered, "No. She said that if she were "substantially involved in any issue while working as the Solicitor General," she would recuse herself. However, the statute does not require "substantial" participation – she added the word "substantial."

Here is what we currently know about her "participation as counsel" concerning ObamaCare. Kagan admitted in writing attending at least one meeting in which Obama's lawyers discussed how to defend ObamaCare against claims that it was unconstitutional. However, she minimizes the extent of the discussion and her participation thereafter.

However, there is good reason to doubt her minimalistic characterizations. While the Justice Department has been generally uncooperative with Congressional requests for more information, some information has come to light that casts serious doubt on Kagan's claims of minimal involvement. Kagan received a number of e-mails that were discussions among Obama's top lawyers about how to defend ObamaCare. Additionally, e-mail records revealed that Kagan said she wanted her office to be a part of these discussions. On March 21 2010, Kagan and her deputy, Neal Katyal, had an extended e-mail exchange whose subject line was "Health care litigation meeting" and said, "It sounds like we can meet with some of the health care policy team tomorrow at 4 to help us prepare for litigation... I think you should go, no? I will, regardless, but feel like this is litigation of singular importance." And when her deputy got specific about whether Kagan should attend, Kagan cut off the e-mail communication and responded, "What's your phone number?" Katyal sent his phone number and the e-mail communication stopped. Interesting that she didn't want an e-mail record of this part of the conversation.

That same day, Ms. Kagan responded to an e-mail from Laurence H. Tribe with the subject line "fingers and toes crossed today!" Ms. Kagan expressed great enthusiasm for ObamaCare, "I hear they have the votes, Larry!! Simply amazing." Note the two exclamation points! Sounds like she's pretty jazzed about the likely passage of ObamaCare.

Two weeks after the Senate passage of ObamaCare, a senior counsel at the Justice Department emailed Kagan's deputy, Katyal, to suggest putting together "a group to get thinking about how to defend against the inevitable challenges to the health care proposals that are pending." Katyal's reply e-mail said, "Absolutely right on. Let's crush them. I'll speak to Elena [Kagan] and designate someone." Later that day, Katyal responded again via e-mail: "Elena would definitely like OSG [Office of the Solicitor General] to be involved in this set of issues. I will handle this myself ... and will bring in Elena as needed."

[13] http://obamacarefacts.com/obamacare-myths.php

[14] Obamacare exchange sends couple voter registration form pre-marked as Democrat By Howard Portnoy on March 30, 2014 at 10:04 am From <http://libertyunyielding.com/2014/03/30/couple-receives-voter-registration-form-pre-marked-democratic-obamacare-exchange/>

[15] http://obamacarefacts.com/obamacare-myths.php

[16] http://www.cruz.senate.gov/files/documents/The%20Legal%20Limit/The%20Legal%20Limit%20Report%204.pdf

[17] http://www.cruz.senate.gov/files/documents/The%20Legal%20Limit/The%20Legal%20

Limit%20Report%204.pdf Margaret Talev & Alex Wayne, Obama Lifts Health Mandate for Those With Canceled Plans, Bloomberg.com, Dec. 20, 2013

18 http://www.cruz.senate.gov/files/documents/The%20Legal%20Limit/The%20Legal%20Limit%20Report%204.pdf ObamaCare's Secret Mandate Exemption , Wall St. J., Mar. 11, 2014.

19 http://www.cruz.senate.gov/files/documents/The%20Legal%20Limit/The%20Legal%20Limit%20Report%204.pdf Stephanie Condon, Obama letting people keep canceled health plans for another year , CBSNews.com, Nov. 14, 2013.

20 http://www.cruz.senate.gov/files/documents/The%20Legal%20Limit/The%20Legal%20Limit%20Report%204.pdf Louise Radnofsky, Obama Gives Health Plans Added Two-Year Reprieve, Wall St. J., Mar. 5, 2014.

21 http://www.cruz.senate.gov/files/documents/The%20Legal%20Limit/The%20Legal%20Limit%20Report%204.pdf David Martosko, Busted! After promising 'no delay' in final Obamacare sign-up deadline, Obama administration unveils new 'honor system' extension through mid-April, Daily Mail, March 25, 2014.

22 http://www.cruz.senate.gov/files/documents/The%20Legal%20Limit/The%20Legal%20Limit%20Report%204.pdf Sarah Kliff, White House delays employer mandate requirement until 2015, Wash. Post, July 2, 2013.

23 http://www.cruz.senate.gov/files/documents/The%20Legal%20Limit/The%20Legal%20Limit%20Report%204.pdf Juliet Eilperin & Amy Goldstein, White House delays health insurance mandate for medium-seized employers until 2016, Wash. Post, Feb. 10, 2014.

24 http://www.cruz.senate.gov/files/documents/The%20Legal%20Limit/The%20Legal%20Limit%20Report%204.pdf Ezra Klein, In 2014, Congress gets Obamacare. Here's how they'll pay for it., Wash. Post, Aug. 1, 2013.

25 http://www.cruz.senate.gov/files/documents/The%20Legal%20Limit/The%20Legal%20Limit%20Report%204.pdf Avik Roy, Yet Another White House Obamacare Delay: Out-Of-Pocket Caps Waived Until 2015, Forbes, Aug. 13, 2013

26 http://www.cruz.senate.gov/files/documents/The%20Legal%20Limit/The%20Legal%20Limit%20Report%204.pdf Avik Roy, Not Qualified for Obamacare's Subsidies? Just lie –Govt. To Use 'Honor System' Without Verifying Your Eligibility, Forbes, July 6, 2013.

27 http://www.cruz.senate.gov/files/documents/The%20Legal%20Limit/The%20Legal%20Limit%20Report%204.pdf Joel Gehrke, Little Sisters of the Poor sue over Obamacare fines, contraception requirement, Wash. Examiner, Sept. 24, 2013.

28 http://www.cruz.senate.gov/files/documents/The%20Legal%20Limit/The%20Legal%20Limit%20Report%204.pdf Milton Wolf, Obamacare waiver corruption must stop, Wash. Times, May 20, 2011.

29 Dictator Obama Threatens Supreme Court Over ObamaCare http://www.canadafreepress.com/index.php/article/46448

30 U.S. Constitution, Article II, Section 3, Clause 5.

31 Timeline of Major Health-Reform Delays 28 Delays, and Counting, to Health Reform By Elizabeth MacDonald Emac's Bottom Line Published February 12, 2014,

FOXBusiness From <http://www.foxbusiness.com/economy-policy/2014/02/12/28-delays-and-counting-to-health-reform/>

[32] http://www.foxnews.com/opinion/2014/02/06/executive-order-tyranny-obama-plans-to-rule-america-with-pen-phone/

[33] From <http://townhall.com/tipsheet/guybenson/2014/03/12/whoa-wh-basically-suspends-individual-mandate-tax-until-2016-n1807920>

[34] House Votes to Delay Obamacare Individual Mandate for a Decade Katie Pavlich | Mar 14, 2014 From <http://townhall.com/tipsheet/katiepavlich/2014/03/14/house-votes-to-delay-obamacare-for-a-decade-n1809180?utm_source=thdailypm&utm_medium=email&utm_campaign=nl_pm>: From <http://townhall.com/tipsheet/guybenson/2014/03/12/whoa-wh-basically-suspends-individual-mandate-tax-until-2016-n1807920>

[35] Obama Admin Slips in Major Obamacare Exemption Quietly Added for Individual Mandate – Seems to Apply to Everyone Lily Dane March 13, 2014 From <http://freedomoutpost.com/2014/03/obama-admin-slips-major-obamacare-exemption-quietly-added-individual-mandate-seems-apply-everyone/>

[36] http://www.foxnews.com/politics/2014/01/19/white-house-reportedly-delays-obamacare-equal-coverage-provision/

[37] Obama to Hispanics: 'Immigration People' Won't Deport Relatives If You Enroll in Obamacare 19 March 2014 <http://minutemennews.com/2014/03/obama-hispanics-immigration-people-wont-deport-relatives-enroll-obamacare/>

[38] Legislative history

*Introduced in the House as the "Service Members Home Ownership Tax Act of 2009" (H.R. 3590) by Charles Rangel (D–NY) on September 17, 2009

*Committee consideration by: Ways and Means

*Passed the House on October 8, 2009 (416–0)

*Passed the Senate as the "Patient Protection and Affordable Care Act" on December 24, 2009 (60–39) with amendment

*House agreed to Senate amendment on March 21, 2010 (219–212)

*Signed into law by President Barack Obama on March 23, 2010

[39] There are 7 versions of Bill Number H.R.3590 for the 111th Congress. Usually, the last item is the most recent.

1 . Service Members Home Ownership Tax Act of 2009 (Introduced in House - IH)[H.R.3590.IH][PDF]

2 . Service Members Home Ownership Tax Act of 2009 (Engrossed in House [Passed House] - EH)[H.R.3590.EH][PDF]

3 . Service Members Home Ownership Tax Act of 2009 (Placed on Calendar Senate - PCS)[H.R.3590.PCS][PDF]

4 . Patient Protection and Affordable Care Act (Amendment in Senate - AS)[H.R.3590.AS][PDF]

5 . Patient Protection and Affordable Care Act (Public Print - PP)[H.R.3590.PP][PDF]

6 . Patient Protection and Affordable Care Act (Engrossed Amendment Senate - EAS)[H.R.3590.EAS][PDF]

7 . Patient Protection and Affordable Care Act (Enrolled Bill [Final as Passed Both House and Senate] - ENR)[H.R.3590.ENR][PDF]

[40] The summary below was written by the Congressional Research Service, which is a nonpartisan division of the Library of Congress. 3/21/2010--Passed House without amendment. (This measure has not been amended since it was introduced. The summary has been expanded because action occurred on the measure.) Sets forth the rule for consideration of the Senate amendments to the bill (H.R. 3590) to amend the Internal

Revenue Code to modify the first-time homebuyers credit in the case of members of the Armed Forces and certain other federal employees, and for other purposes, and providing for consideration of the bill (H.R. 4872) to provide for reconciliation pursuant to section 202 of the concurrent resolution on the budget for FY2010. Makes it in order to consider a single motion offered by the Majority Leader or a designee that the House concur in the Senate amendments to H.R. 3590 without intervention of any point of order except those arising under clause 10 of Rule XXI. Provides, upon adoption of the motion to concur in the Senate amendments, for a closed rule for consideration of H.R. 4872. Waives all points of order against consideration of H.R. 4872 except those arising under clause 10 of Rule XXI. Provides that the amendment in the nature of a substitute printed in part A of the Rules Committee report accompanying this resolution, modified by the amendment printed in part B of the report, shall be considered as adopted and the bill, as amended, shall be considered as read. Waives all points of order against H.R. 4872, as amended. Provides one motion to recommit the bill with or without instructions. Provides that until completion of the proceedings described above: (1) the Chair may decline to entertain any intervening motion, resolution, question, or notice, decline to entertain the question of consideration, and may postpone proceedings to a time designated by the Speaker; (2) the second sentence of clause 1(a) of Rule XIX (regarding 40 minutes of debate on questions not debated) shall not apply; and (3) any proposition admissible under the proceedings described in this resolution shall be considered as read. From <https://www.govtrack.us/congress/bills/111/hres1203#summary>

[41] H.Res. 1203 (111th):The summary below was written by the Congressional Research Service, which is a nonpartisan division of the Library of Congress. 3/21/2010--Passed House without amendment. (This measure has not been amended since it was introduced. The summary has been expanded because action occurred on the measure.) Sets forth the rule for consideration of the Senate amendments to the bill (H.R. 3590) to amend the Internal Revenue Code to modify the first-time homebuyers credit in the case of members of the Armed Forces and certain other federal employees, and for other purposes, and providing for consideration of the bill (H.R. 4872) to provide for reconciliation pursuant to section 202 of the concurrent resolution on the budget for FY2010. Makes it in order to consider a single motion offered by the Majority Leader or a designee that the House concur in the Senate amendments to H.R. 3590 without intervention of any point of order except those arising under clause 10 of Rule XXI. Provides, upon adoption of the motion to concur in the Senate amendments, for a closed rule for consideration of H.R. 4872. Waives all points of order against consideration of H.R. 4872 except those arising under clause 10 of Rule XXI. Provides that the amendment in the nature of a substitute printed in part A of the Rules Committee report accompanying this resolution, modified by the amendment printed in part B of the report, shall be considered as adopted and the bill, as amended, shall be considered as read. Waives all points of order against H.R. 4872, as amended. Provides one motion to recommit the bill with or without instructions. Provides that until completion of the proceedings described above: (1) the Chair may decline to entertain any intervening motion, resolution, question, or notice, decline to entertain the question of consideration, and may postpone proceedings to a time designated by the Speaker; (2) the second sentence of clause 1(a) of Rule XIX (regarding 40 minutes of debate on questions not debated) shall not apply; and (3) any proposition admissible under the proceedings described in this resolution shall be considered as read. From <https://www.govtrack.us/congress/bills/111/hres1203#summary>

[42] From <http://www.nationalreview.com/articles/280274/reconciliation-option-james-c-capretta>

[43] Decoding the Obama Health Law: What you Need to know - Betsy McCaughey location 1195

[44] FINAL VOTE RESULTS

FOR ROLL CALL 165

(Democrats in roman; Republicans in *italic*; Independents underlined)

H R 3590 RECORDED VOTE 21-Mar-2010 10:49 PM

QUESTION: On Motion to Concur in Senate Amendments

BILL TITLE: Patient Protection and Affordable Care Act

	Ayes	Noes	PRES	NV
Democratic	219	34		
Republican	0	178		
Independent	0	0		
TOTALS	219	212		

[45] Required: Simple Majority Passed by 51%

House Vote 167	Ayes	Noes	PRES	NV
Democratic	220	33		
Republican	0	178		
Independent				
TOTALS	220	211		

https://www.govtrack.us/congress/votes/111-2010/h167

[46] AMENDMENT NO. 2786

Purpose: In the nature of a substitute.

IN THE SENATE OF THE UNITED STATES—111th Cong., 1st Sess. H. R. 3590

To amend the Internal Revenue Code of 1986 to modify the first-time homebuyers credit in the case of members of the Armed Forces and certain other Federal employees, and for other purposes.

November 19, 2009

Ordered to lie on the table and to be printed

Amendment in the nature of a substitute intended to be

proposed by Mr. REID (for himself, Mr. BAUCUS, Mr. DODD, and Mr. HARKIN)

Viz:

Strike all after the enacting clause and insert the following:

SECTION 1. SHORT TITLE; TABLE OF CONTENTS.

3(a) SHORT TITLE

.—This Act may be cited as the ''Patient Protection and Affordable Care Act''.

[47] Pelosi Plots End Run to Pass Obamacare By David A. Patten Tuesday, 16 Mar 2010 http://www.newsmax.com/InsideCover/pelosi-healthcare-vote-democrats/2010/03/16/id/352913#ixzz2jL39PuVz

[48] *Wayman v. Southard* (1825)

[49] 276 U.S. 394 (1928) at 406

[50] http://www.breitbart.com/Big-Government/2013/03/01/HHS-Releases-More-Than-700-Pages-of-New-Obamacare-Rules

[51] Citizens' Council on Health Care http://www.cchfreedom.org/pdf/ObamaCareCzar.pdf

[52] http://www.gop.gov/blog/10/02/25/159-ways-the-senate-bill

[53] Decoding the Obama Health Law: What you Need to know - Betsy McCaughey Read more at location 929

[54] H. R. 3590—664 (starting to list all agencies and departments for sharing of information)

''(d) The Secretary may promulgate a regulation that provides an evidentiary privilege for, and provides for the confidentiality of communications between or among, any of the following entities or their agents, consultants, or employees:

'(1) A State insurance department.
''(2) A State attorney general.
''(3) The National Association of Insurance Commissioners.
''(4) The Department of Labor.
''(5) The Department of the Treasury.
''(6) The Department of Justice.
''(7) The Department of Health and Human Services.
''(8) Any other Federal or State authority that the Secretary determines is appropriate for the purposes of enforcing the provisions of this title.

[55] From <http://spectator.org/articles/39516/empress-obamacare>

[56] http://www.recovery.gov/arra/Accountability/Documents/NonCompliers_Q42013.pdf ; From <http://washingtonexaminer.com/recipients-of-stimulus-funds-fail-to-report-what-they-do-with-the-money/article/2544285>

[57] http://hotair.com/archives/2014/01/15/federal-judge-no-the-obamacare-statute-doesnt-limit-subsidies-to-state-run-exchanges/ "Section 1311 of the law authorizes the states to develop their own ObamaCare exchanges. Section 1321 says that, if a state declines, the feds can step in and develop their own exchange for consumers in that state instead. That's how we ended up with the technological marvel that is Healthcare.gov. The rub comes in Section 1401, which authorizes tax credits, i.e. premium subsidies, for anyone who's in "an Exchange established by the State under 1311". Wait a sec — does that mean that only people enrolled in state-run exchanges get subsidies? If people enrolled in the federal exchange get them too, why doesn't Section 1401 say "an Exchange established by the State under 1311 *or the federal government under section 1321*"?"

[58] Could This Be The End Of Obamacare? A decision is supposed to come in late June, and looks like it will be in favor of the plaintiffs. Roger Aranoff — March 28, 2014 From <http://www.westernjournalism.com/obamacares-tough-day-court/>

[59] https://www.thefederalistpapers.org/principles-of-constitutional-interpretation

[60] http://hotair.com/archives/2014/01/15/federal-judge-no-the-obamacare-statute-doesnt-limit-subsidies-to-state-run-exchanges/ "

[61] *Bill: Reconciliation Act; Page: 108-113* From <http://www.atr.org/full-list-obamacare-tax-hikes-listed-a7010#ixzz1zTXuZUYl>

[62] From <http://hotair.com/archives/2014/02/13/irs-obamacare-self-attestation-for-businesses-adding-irrationality-to-lawlessness/>

[63] *Id.*

[64] Compilation of entities that received money under this program:
Commercial Organizations (834) received $1,779,774,095 - 37.8%
Governmental Entities (1,326) received $2,100,337,403 - 44.6%
Unions (495) received $781,209,744 - 16.6%
Nonprofit Organizations (139) received $40,006,145 - 0.8%
Others (5) received $12,940,130 - 0.3%
Total $4,714,267,517
Recipients and amount received:
State of New Jersey Treasury Department $98,606,767
Commonwealth of Kentucky $95,474,718
State of New York $88,424,151
Board of Trustees of North Carolina Teachers' and State Employees' Comprehensive Major Medical Plan $87,462,204
State Teachers Retirement System of Ohio $78,693,323
State of Michigan Public School Employees Retirement System $64,379,629
National Carriers' Conference Committee $60,016,187
Georgia Department of Community Health $57,936,127
Commonwealth of Massachusetts $51,311,601

The Boeing Company $50,160,905
State of Michigan $46,936,210
Alcatel-Lucent USA Inc. $42,438,274
United Parcel Service of America, Inc. $37,394,549
Commonwealth of Pennsylvania $32,192,146
Public Education Employees Health Insurance Fund—Alabama $32,040,120
Employees Retirement System of Texas (ERS) $30,175,627
State of Alaska Retirement and Benefits Plans $27,637,600 0.6%
South Carolina Budget & Control Board, Employee Insurance Program $27,142,502
Arizona State Retirement System $19,977,697
Department of Finance and Administration—Mississippi $19,890,691
Oregon Educators Benefit Board $19,446,347
The Boeing Company $50,160,905
Alcatel-Lucent USA Inc. $42,438,274
General Motors LLC $31,282,424
International Business Machines Corporation (IBM) $30,963,516
Deere & Company $28,083,767
Delta Air Lines, Inc. $27,309,420
American Airlines Inc. $24,260,058
Qwest Communications International Inc. $23,584,496
Pfizer Inc. $23,001,263
Caterpillar Inc. $20,335,732
The Procter & Gamble Company $19,186,151
Alcoa Inc. $17,404,025
Ford Motor Company $17,290,036
The Dow Chemical Company $16,255,671
BP Corporation North America Inc. $16,179,320
E.I. DuPont de Nemours and Company $15,401,279
National Carriers' Conference Committee $60,016,187
Wisconsin Education Association Insurance Trust $33,459,558
SISC III Health & Welfare $27,492,509
Trustees of the Central States, SE & SW Areas H&W Fund—Illinois $22,716,745
Joint Plan Committee—Delaware $14,803,314 0.3%
Steelworkers Health and Welfare Fund $12,503,419
Maine Education Association Benefits Trust $8,862,203
UFCW & Employers Benefit Trust $8,825,664
Boilermakers National Health and Welfare Fund $7,668,334
National Automatic Sprinkler Industry Welfare Fund Joint Board of Trustees $6,956,390
Michigan Conference of Teamsters Welfare Fund $6,040,715
Chicago District Council of Carpenters Welfare Fund $5,164,412
Pension, Hospitalization and Benefit Plan of the Electrical Industry $4,920,494
Governing Committee—Delaware $4,600,801
1199 SEIU National Benefit Fund for Health and Human Service Employees $4,359,989
Management–Ila Managed Health Care Trust Fund $4,291,264
Insurance and Benefits Trust of Peace Officers Research Association of California $3,207,969
Screen Actors Guild–Producers Health Plan $3,049,896
Midwest Operating Engineers Welfare Fund $2,999,218
Nonprofit recipients:
Blue Cross Blue Shield of Michigan $3,713,920
Kaiser Foundation Health Plan, Inc. $948,844
President and Fellows of Harvard College $929,113

Independence Blue Cross $746,570
Yale University $713,799
Trustees of Princeton University $706,165
Duke University $604,797
Chandler Health Care Benefits Trust $574,218
Eastern Maine Healthcare Systems $484,937
Massachusetts Institute of Technology $481,345
Cornell University $472,607
Community Hospital of the Monterey Peninsula $463,760
New York University $454,544
Read more at http://freedomoutpost.com/2013/10/obamacare-appropriations-billions-taxpayer-dollars-werent-told-even-passed-law/#k2JeKF6XFxlEOMsU.99

65 http://townhall.com/tipsheet/guybenson/2013/03/12/photo-20000-pages-of-obamacare-regulations-n1532069

66 http://freedomoutpost.com/2014/02/nullification-yes-can/

67 Missouri House Moving on Health Care Nullification Act Read more: http://freedomoutpost.com/2013/03/obama-ignores-nullification-says-federal-agents-will-enforce-obamacare/#ixzz2OeZmCsRz

68 Georgia House Votes to Nullify Obamacare Tim Brown 15 hours ago Late Monday evening, the Georgia State House of Representatives passed HB707, which bans the state participating in significant portions of the Affordable Care Act, aka Obamacare. The vote was 115-59.

69 Ohio Constitution Stops Obamacare in its Tracks! Posted By Lorri Anderson on Jan 11, 2014 Read more at http://freedomoutpost.com/2014/01/good-news-ohio-constitution-stops-obamacare-tracks/#Y0wyt4mrhyQLjkkm.99

70 Missouri House Moving on Health Care Nullification Act Read more: http://freedomoutpost.com/2013/03/obama-ignores-nullification-says-federal-agents-will-enforce-obamacare/#ixzz2OeZmCsRz

71 From <http://www.foxnews.com/politics/2014/01/07/vermont-backs-controversial-single-payer-system-for-health-care-overhaul-but/>

72 BEYOND REPAIR: Maryland expected to ditch $125M ObamaCare exchange 3/29/14 From <http://www.foxnews.com/>

73 Obamacare "Beneficiary:" I've Been Rejected by 96 Doctors So Far Guy Benson | Apr 09, 2014 http://townhall.com/tipsheet/guybenson/2014/04/09/obamacare-beneficiary-ive-been-rejected-by-96-doctors-so-far-n1822166?utm_source=thdaily&utm_medium=email&utm_campaign=nl

74 Washington Rejects Obama's Proposal to Extend Canceled Policies - Unwilling & Unable http://freedomoutpost.com/2013/11/washington-rejects-obamas-proposal-extend-canceled-policies-unwilling-unable/#disqus_thread

75 HR 3950 Pg. 791 (b)(1) Section 5000A(b)(1) of the Internal Revenue Code of 1986, as added by section 1501(b) of this Act, is amended to read as follows:

> '(1) IN GENERAL- If a taxpayer who is an applicable individual, or an applicable individual for whom the taxpayer is liable under paragraph (3), fails to meet the requirement of subsection (a) for 1 or more months, then, except as provided in subsection (e), there is hereby imposed on the taxpayer a penalty with respect to such failures in the amount determined under subsection (c).'.
>
> (2) Paragraphs (1) and (2) of section 5000A(c) of the Internal Revenue Code of 1986, as so added, are amended to read as follows:
>
> '(1) IN GENERAL- The amount of the penalty imposed by this section on any taxpayer for any taxable year with respect to failures described in subsection (b)(1) shall be equal to the lesser of--

'(A) the sum of the monthly penalty amounts determined under paragraph (2) for months in the taxable year during which 1 or more such failures occurred, or

'(B) an amount equal to the national average premium for qualified health plans which have a bronze level of coverage, provide coverage for the applicable family size involved, and are offered through Exchanges for plan years beginning in the calendar year with or within which the taxable year ends.

'(2) MONTHLY PENALTY AMOUNTS- For purposes of paragraph (1)(A), the monthly penalty amount with respect to any taxpayer for any month during which any failure described in subsection (b)(1) occurred is an amount equal to 1/12 of the greater of the following amounts:

'(A) FLAT DOLLAR AMOUNT- An amount equal to the lesser of--

'(i) the sum of the applicable dollar amounts for all individuals with respect to whom such failure occurred during such month, or

'(ii) 300 percent of the applicable dollar amount (determined without regard to paragraph (3)(C)) for the calendar year with or within which the taxable year ends.

'(B) PERCENTAGE OF INCOME- An amount equal to the following percentage of the taxpayer's household income for the taxable year:CommentsPermalink

'(i) 0.5 percent for taxable years beginning in 2014.

'(ii) 1.0 percent for taxable years beginning in 2015.

'(iii) 2.0 percent for taxable years beginning after 2015.'.

[76] Sources:US Code 2011, Title 26, subtitle D, Chapter 48, sec5000A; IRS: Questions and Answers on the Individual Shared Responsibility Provision; Congressional Research Service report: Individual Mandate and Related Information Requirements Under the PPACA

[77] Forbes, How Much Does Obamacare Rip Off Young Adults? We Ran The Numbers. Here Are The Results. Dr. Scott Gottlieb http://www.forbes.com/sites/scottgottlieb/2014/03/28/how-much-does-obamacare-rip-off-generation-x-we-ran-the-numbers-here-are-the-results/ "My AEI colleague Kelly Funderburk and I looked at four states: Arizona, Illinois, Pennsylvania, and Texas. We then looked at a typical 30-year-old at one of six different annual income brackets: $20,000 in annual income, $25K, $30K, $35K, $40K, and $45K. For each of the four states, we computed how much an Aetna AET +0.2% Classic Silver plan would cost the same 30-year-old at each of these six income bands. We looked at monthly premiums, deductibles, and out of pocket limits. We chose the Aetna plan because it is generally considered a higher quality insurance, operated across all of these markets, and represented a median price point among the offerings."

[78] ObamaCare Survival Guide by Nicholas J. Tate, location 523

[79] *Id.* at location 2463

[80] The Truth About Obamacare (Sally C. Pipes)- Highlight Loc. 233-34

[81] Five major ObamaCare taxes that will hit your wallet in 2013, By John Kartch Published July 05, 2012 FoxNews.com

[82] Decoding the Obama Health Law: What you Need to know - Betsy McCaughey, location 795
[83] National Tax on insurance companies $2/person insured HR 3950 Pg 625
[84] Decoding the Obama Health Law: What you Need to know - Betsy McCaughey, location 814
[85] Insurance Company Lays Out Obamacare Tax Hikes Kevin Glass | Dec 27, 2013 From <http://townhall.com/tipsheet/kevinglass/2013/12/27/insurance-company-lays-out-obamacare-tax-hikes-n1768729?utm_source=thdailypm&utm_medium=email&utm_campaign=nl_pm>
[86] The Truth About Obamacare (Sally C. Pipes)- Loc. 2462
[87] http://www.usinflationcalculator.com/
[88] Robert Allen Bonelli Breitbart.com from <http://freedomoutpost.com/2012/06/20-additional-taxes-under-obamacare/>
[89] *Id.*
[90] *Id.*
[91] HR 3905, SEC. 9017
[92] Full List of Obamacare Tax Hikes: Listed by Size of Tax Hike, From <http://www.atr.org/full-list-obamacare-tax-hikes-listed-a7010#ixzz1zTXuZUYl> *Bill: PPACA; Page: 345-346*
[93] Full List of Obamacare Tax Hikes: Listed by Size of Tax Hike, *Bill: Reconciliation Act; Page: 108-113* From <http://www.atr.org/full-list-obamacare-tax-hikes-listed-a7010#ixzz1zTXuZUYl>
[94] *Id.* at Bill: PPACA; Page: 317-337
[95] Health Contract with America John C. Goodman Jul 07, 2012
[96] *Id.*
[97] *Id.*
[98] potentially paid by the above average US citizen, 2013 est. - 59.7% http://www.nowandfutures.com/taxes.html
[99] The Truth About Obamacare (Sally C. Pipes)- Highlight Loc. 287-90
[100] *Id.* at Loc. 287-90
[101] *Id.* at Loc. 314-17
[102] *Id.* at Loc. 318-19
[103] *Id.* at Loc. 426-28
[104] http://www.forbes.com/sites/sallypipes/2011/12/19/the-ugly-realities-of-socialized-medicine-are-not-going-away-3/
[105] *Id.*
[106] *Id.*
[107] The Truth About Obamacare (Sally C. Pipes)- Highlight Loc. 329-30
[108] *Id.* at Loc. 332
[109] *Id.* at Loc. 342-43
[110] http://conservativeamericaonline.blogspot.com/2012/06/doctor-claims-nhs-killing-off-130000.html#more; http://conservativeamericaonline.blogspot.com/2013/02/yet-another-obamacare-nightmare-to-come.html?utm_source=America%27s+Conservative+News&utm_campaign=d91ba1a128-RSS_EMAIL_CAMPAIGN&utm_medium=email#more
[111] Woman Denied Medical Care Because Her Carbon Footprint Is Too Big, April 12, 2012, CanadaFreePress.com http://conservativeamericaonline.blogspot.com/2012/04/woman-denied-medical-care-because-her.html#more
[112] The Truth About Obamacare (Sally C. Pipes)- Highlight Loc. 334-36
[113] *Id.*
[114] *Id.* at 365-67

[115] *Id.* at Loc. 367-70
[116] *Id.* at Loc. 386-87
[117] *Id.* at Page 200
[118] *Id.* at Page 201
[119] *Id.*
[120] ObamaCare Survival Guide by Nicholas J. Tate location 1299-1309
[121] Obamacare "Beneficiary:" I've Been Rejected by 96 Doctors So Far Guy Benson | Apr 09, 2014 http://townhall.com/tipsheet/guybenson/2014/04/09/obamacare-beneficiary-ive-been-rejected-by-96-doctors-so-far-n1822166?utm_source=thdaily&utm_medium=email&utm_campaign=nl
[122] http://www.breitbart.com/Big-Government/2014/04/16/Brain-Surgery-Patient-s-Obamacare-Plan-Denies-Meds-Drops-Doctors
[123] Obamacare "Beneficiary:" I've Been Rejected by 96 Doctors So Far Guy Benson | Apr 09, 2014 http://townhall.com/tipsheet/guybenson/2014/04/09/obamacare-beneficiary-ive-been-rejected-by-96-doctors-so-far-n1822166?utm_source=thdaily&utm_medium=email&utm_campaign=nl
[124] *Id.*
[125] *Id.*
[126] *Id.*
[127] Vegas man stuck with $407,000 medical bill after ObamaCare breakdown Published March 18, 2014 FoxNews.com From <http://www.foxnews.com/politics/2014/03/18/vegas-man-stuck-with-407000-medical-bill-after-obamacare-breakdown/>
[128] Nation's top cancer hospitals not covered under Obamacare By Howard Portnoy on March 20, 2014 at 11:42 am From <http://libertyunyielding.com/2014/03/20/nations-top-cancer-hospitals-covered-obamacare/>
[129] *Id.*
[130] Awful: Cancer Patient Discovers Recent Surgery Wasn't Covered Under Obamacare Plan Guy Benson | Mar 06, 2014 http://townhall.com/tipsheet/guybenson/2014/03/06/awful-cancer-patient-discovers-recent-surgery-wasnt-covered-under-obamacare-plan-n1804587?utm_source=thdailypm&utm_medium=email&utm_campaign=nl_pm
[131] http://www.foxnews.com/health/2014/02/02/veterans-dying-because-treatment-delays-at-va-hospitals-document-says/
[132] Reports of erroneous WA health exchange debits - (Give Government your Bank account number and it is the gift that keeps on giving) by ELISA HAHN / KING 5 News Posted on December 10, 2013 at 8:28 AM From <http://www.kgw.com/news/Enrollees-report-erroneous-debits-by-WA-Healthplanfinder-235244701.html>
[133] Decoding the Obama Health Law: What you Need to know - Betsy McCaughey Read more at location 581
[134] Why the UK Is Ditching Socialized Medicine February 20, 2012 by Arnold Ahlert http://www.frontpagemag.com/2012/arnold-ahlert/why-the-uk-is-ditching-socialized-medicine
[135] *Id.*
[136] *Id.*
[137] *Id.*
[138] *Id.*
[139] Michael Cannon, Director of Health Policy Studies at the non-partisan Cato Institute, offered testimony before the OGR Committee.
[140] How the government spent $394 MILLION on the Obamacare website - more than it cost to build Facebook and Twitter - and it STILL doesn't work
[141] Maryland Obamacare exchange spent $90 million on technology before abandoning

website 8:54 PM 04/18/2014 Sarah Hurtubise
http://dailycaller.com/2014/04/18/maryland-obamacare-exchange-spent-90-million-on-technology-before-abandoning-website/#ixzz2zLbekOrG
[142] *Id.*
[143] http://www.katu.com/news/investigators/Cover-Oregon-allegation-if-its-true-someones-going-to-prison-243427781.html

144 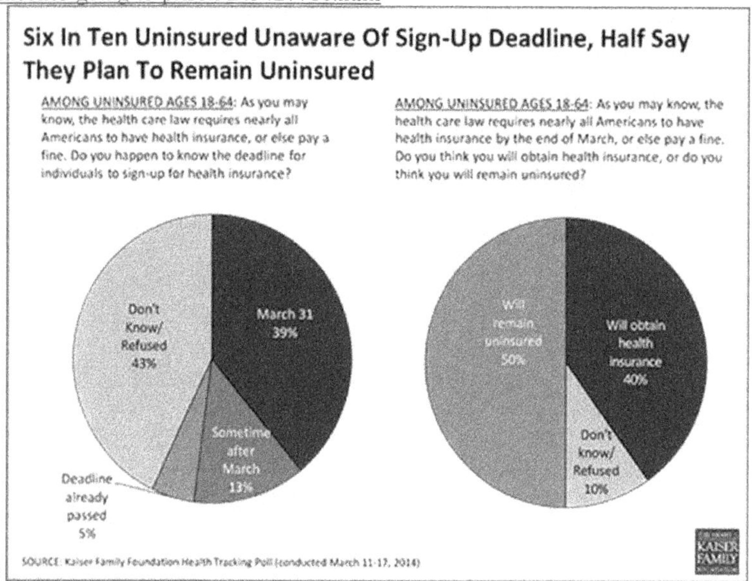

[145] Obamacare exchange sends couple voter registration form pre-marked as Democrat By Howard Portnoy on March 30, 2014 at 10:04 am From <http://libertyunyielding.com/2014/03/30/couple-receives-voter-registration-form-pre-marked-democratic-obamacare-exchange/>
[146] Obamacare exchange sends couple voter registration form pre-marked as Democrat By Howard Portnoy on March 30, 2014 at 10:04 am From <http://libertyunyielding.com/2014/03/30/couple-receives-voter-registration-form-pre-marked-democratic-obamacare-exchange/> Section 7 of the Act requires states to offer voter registration opportunities at all offices that provide public assistance and all offices that provide state-funded programs primarily engaged in providing services to persons with disabilities. Each applicant for any of these services, renewal of services, or address changes must be provided with a voter registration form of a declination form as well as assistance in completing the form and forwarding the completed application to the appropriate state or local election official. [Emphasis added] Whether a website can reasonably be called an "office" is open to debate. What is not debatable is the illegality of selecting a party affiliation for private citizens.
[147] Video: No, the Obamacare Debate is Not "Over" Guy Benson | Apr 21, 2014 http://townhall.com/tipsheet/guybenson/2014/04/21/no-the-obamacare-debate-and-irs-scandal-arent-over-n1826827?utm_source=thdailypm&utm_medium=email&utm_campaign=nl_pm
[148] *Id.*
[149] Georgia exchange applications hit 220,000 By: Andy Miller Published: Apr 16, 2014 http://www.georgiahealthnews.com/2014/04/georgia-exchange-applications-hit-220000/#sthash.f7koLgjp.dpuf
[150] *Id.*

[151] According to Heather Ginsberg, a major part of Healthcare.gov are still not working properly is the "function that accurately pays insurers."
[152] Much of Healthcare.gov is Still Under Construction Heather Ginsberg | Apr 27, 2014 http://townhall.com/tipsheet/heatherginsberg/2014/04/27/much-of-healthcaregov-is-still-under-construction-n1829662?utm_source=thdaily&utm_medium=email&utm_campaign=nl
[153] Corrupt as Chicago: Judicial Watch Sues HHS for Obamacare Navigator Records Katie Pavlich | Apr 22, 2014 http://townhall.com/tipsheet/katiepavlich/2014/04/22/judicial-watch-sues-hhs-for-obamacare-navigator-records-n1827493?utm_source=thdailypm&utm_medium=email&utm_campaign=nl_pm And From <http://capitolcityproject.com/confidential-obamacare-navigator-training-manual-uploaded-online-2/>
[154] WOW: Obamacare Navigators Caught On Tape Encouraging Lying On Applications Christine Rousselle | Nov 11, 2013
[155] BREAKING: New Report Says Obamacare Navigator Program Marred by Mismanagement, Confusion Guy Benson | Dec 16, 2013 From <http://townhall.com/tipsheet/guybenson/2013/12/16/report-obamacare-navigator-program-marred-by-mismanagement-confusion-n1763342?utm_source=thdaily&utm_medium=email&utm_campaign=nl>
[156] Corrupt as Chicago: Judicial Watch Sues HHS for Obamacare Navigator Records Katie Pavlich | Apr 22, 2014 http://townhall.com/tipsheet/katiepavlich/2014/04/22/judicial-watch-sues-hhs-for-obamacare-navigator-records-n1827493?utm_source=thdailypm&utm_medium=email&utm_campaign=nl_pm
[157] http://conservativeamericaonline.blogspot.com/2012/07/6500-new-irs-agents-needed-to-provide.html#more
[158] *Id.*
[159] http://www.renewamerica.com/columns/kouri/120704
[160] Ron Paul Warned about an Armed BLM in 1997
Read more at http://freedomoutpost.com/2014/04/ron-paul-warned-armed-blm-1997/#PKXTiX17iUlSD8Eb.99 http://freedomoutpost.com/2014/04/ron-paul-warned-armed-blm-1997/
[161] http://www.gopusa.com/commentary/2011/04/18/barone-president-whatever-finds-things-not-going-his-way/> Barone: President Whatever Finds Things Not Going His Way By Michael Barone April 18, 2011 6:25 am
[162] http://www.theblaze.com/stories/2012/01/06/how-many-businesses-are-exempt-the-final-number-of-obamacare-waivers-is-in/
[163] https://www.askheritage.org/how-about-a-national-obamacare-waiver/ http://www.politifact.com/truth-o-meter/statements/2013/oct/18/mick-mulvaney/rep-mulvaney-says-obama-gave-1100-special-waivers-/ http://www.theblaze.com/stories/2012/01/06/how-many-businesses-are-exempt-the-final-number-of-obamacare-waivers-is-in/
[164] ObamaCare Survival Guide by Nicholas J. Tate location 605
[165] http://www.nationalreview.com/article/355176/congresss-obamacare-waiver-michael-f-cannon
[166] *Id.*
[167] http://www.washingtonpost.com/blogs/fact-checker/wp/2013/10/16/did-obama-exempt-1200-groups-including-congress-from-obamacare/
[168] (c) Section 5000A(d)(2)(A) of the Internal Revenue Code of 1986, as added by section 1501(b) of this Act, is amended to read as follows: ''(A) RELIGIOUS CONSCIENCE EXEMPTION.—Such term shall not include any individual for any month if such

individual has in effect an exemption under section 1311(d)(4)(H) of the Patient Protection and Affordable Care Act which certifies that such individual is— ''(i) a member of a recognized religious sect or division thereof which is described in section 1402(g)(1), and ''(ii) an adherent of established tenets or teachings of such sect or division as described in such section.''.

169 26 U.S.C. § 5000A(d)-(e) (2010).

170 Obama Admin Slips in Major Obamacare Exemption Quietly Added for Individual Mandate – Seems to Apply to Everyone Lily Dane March 13, 2014 From <http://freedomoutpost.com/2014/03/obama-admin-slips-major-obamacare-exemption-quietly-added-individual-mandate-seems-apply-everyone/>

171 Administration faces backlash over new ObamaCare exemptions Published December 20, 2013 FoxNews.com Fox News Ed Henry and The Associated Press contributed to this report From <http://www.foxnews.com/politics/2013/12/20/administration-announces-new-obamacare-exemption/>

172 *Id.*

173 ObamaCare Survival Guide by Nicholas J. Tate location 1831

174 "Effects of the Legislation on Insurance Coverage" CBO and JCT estimate that by 2019, the combined effect of enacting H.R. 3590 and the reconciliation proposal would be to reduce the number of nonelderly people who are uninsured by about 32 million, leaving about 23 million nonelderly residents uninsured (about one-third of whom would be unauthorized immigrants). Under the legislation, the share of legal nonelderly residents with insurance coverage would rise from about 83 percent currently to about 94 percent. Letter to Pelosi from the Congressional Budget Office 3/20/2010 From <http://www.cbo.gov/sites/default/files/cbofiles/ftpdocs/113xx/doc11379/amendreconprop.pdf>

175 ObamaCare's Latest Numbers Don't Add Up. You Will Pay the Difference. Written by Gary North on December 4, 2013 From <http://teapartyeconomist.com/2013/12/04/obamacares-latest-numbers-dont-add-will-pay-difference/>

176 Decoding the Obama Health Law: What you Need to know - Betsy McCaughey Read more at location 596

177 *Id.* at location 597

178 *Id.* at location 1241

179 *Id.* at location 691

180 *Id.* at location 690

181 *Id.* at location 688

182 *Id.* at location 673

183 Read the rest of this Liberty Alliance article here: http://libertyalliance.com/2014/04/latest-obamacare-glitch-dishonoring-americas-elderly/#yEMiTQCguEdrDb58.99

184 ObamaCare Survival Guide by Nicholas J. Tate location 1831

185 ObamaCare price hikes hit 'red states' hardest By Maxim Lott Published November 05, 2013 From <http://www.foxnews.com/politics/2013/11/05/obamacare-price-hikes-hit-red-states-hardest/>

186 http://www.breitbart.com/Big-Government/2014/03/19/Obamacare-Patients-Denied-Access-to-Doctors-Hospitals-Cancer-Centers

187 Read more at http://www.westernjournalism.com/next-four-obamacare-disasters/2/#o2DJAk22OIrVE0u0.99

188 http://townhall.com/tipsheet/guybenson/2014/03/06/awful-cancer-patient-discovers-recent-surgery-wasnt-covered-under-obamacare-plan-n1804587?utm_source=thdailypm&utm_medium=email&utm_campaign=nl_pm

189 From <http://www.foxnews.com/politics/2014/03/18/vegas-man-stuck-with-407000-

medical-bill-after-obamacare-breakdown/>

[190] The Truth About Obamacare (Sally C. Pipes)- Highlight Loc. 1720-22

[191] Union official: Smoking, obesity, other health issues could mean paying more under ObamaCare By Jim Angle Published December 18, 2013 From <http://www.foxnews.com/politics/2013/12/18/smoking-obesity-other-health-issues-can-mean-paying-more-under-obamacare/>

[192] *Id.*

[193] *Id.*

[194] What ObamaCare Is -- and What to Expect Carol Platt Liebau Nov 23, 2013 From <http://townhall.com/tipsheet/carolplattliebau/2013/25/23/what-obamacare-is--and-what-to-expect-n1752135?utm_source=thdaily&utm_medium=email&utm_campaign=nl>

[195] Irony Alert: Union Report Charges ObamaCare with Worsening "Income Inequality" Carol Platt Liebau | Mar 10, 2014 From <http://townhall.com/tipsheet/carolplattliebau/2014/03/10/irony-alert-union-report-charges-obamacare-with-worsening-income-inequality-n1806756?utm_source=thdaily&utm_medium=email&utm_campaign=nl>

[196] Decoding the Obama Health Law: What you Need to know - Betsy McCaughey Read more at location 1395

[197] ACA -Pg 477 - (F) recommendations creating or revising national loan repayment programs and scholarship programs to require low-income, minority medical students to serve in their home communities, if designated as medical underserved community.

[198] FoxNews.com Published April 07, 2014 http://www.foxnews.com/politics/2014/04/07/gallup-survey-suggests-sign-ups-under-obamacare-not-as-high-as-white-house-says/

[199] *Id.*

[200] Decoding the Obama Health Law: What you Need to know - Betsy McCaughey Read more at location 375

[201] United Nations: Denial of Obamacare for Illegal Aliens a 'Human Rights' Concern 29 March 2014 Read more at http://minutemennews.com/2014/03/united-nations-obamacare-illegal-aliens-human-rights-concern/#iXq2ZXjc4WQ6VwV9.99

[202] Decoding the Obama Health Law: What you Need to know - Betsy McCaughey Read more at location 377 and 1378

[203] The Inevitability of Obamacare for Illegal Aliens Michelle Malkin | Mar 05, 2014 http://townhall.com/columnists/michellemalkin/

[204] *Id.* AND Obama to Hispanics: 'Immigration People' Won't Deport Relatives If You Enroll in Obamacare 19 March 2014, Read more at http://minutemennews.com/2014/03/obama-hispanics-immigration-people-wont-deport-relatives-enroll-obamacare/#LXZf32iypsfh3TMX.99

[205] <http://freedomoutpost.com/2013/10/obamacare-appropriations-billions-taxpayer-dollars-werent-told-even-passed-law/>

[206] Obamacare is a Prisoner Rehabilitation Program Too! 11 March 2014 Read more at http://minutemennews.com/2014/03/obamacare-prisoner-rehabilitation-program/#B3UpAu79f8YTC1Ti.99

[207] *Id.*

[208] *Id.*

[209] Reports: More Obamacare Cancellations, Premium Hikes On the Way Guy Benson | May 09, 2014 http://townhall.com/tipsheet/guybenson/2014/05/09/reports-more-obamacare-cancellations-premium-hikes-on-the-way-n1836066?utm_source=thdaily&utm_medium=email&utm_campaign=nl

[210] The Truth About Obamacare (Sally C. Pipes)- Highlight Loc. 1181-87

[211] Pasted from <http://conservativebyte.com/2011/11/obama-seeks-to-circumvent-congress-to-fix-%e2%80%98obamacare-glitch%e2%80%99/> Obama Seeks to

Circumvent Congress to Fix 'Obamacare Glitch' Posted on November 17, 2011 by Conservative Byte

212 From <http://www.forbes.com/sites/theapothecary/2012/08/16/fact-checking-the-obama-campaigns-defense-of-its-716-billion-cut-to-medicare/>

213 The Looming ObamaCare Disaster Dr. Elaina George 17 Aug 2013 From <http://www.breitbart.com/Big-Government/2013/08/11/ObamaCare-Smoke-And-Mirrors> Since 1948, when the United Nations

214 The Truth About Obamacare (Sally C. Pipes)- Highlight Loc. 2569-71

215 *Id.* at Loc. 2571-73

216 *Id.* at Loc. 2571-73

217 David Limbaugh April 19, 2011 Pasted from <http://www.gopusa.com/commentary/2011/04/19/limbaugh-ryan-1-obama-0/>

218 ObamaCare created a Medicaid time bomb By Michael D. Tanner December 7, 2013 | 9:15pm http://nypost.com/2013/12/07/the-medicaid-time-bomb/

219 ObamaCare Survival Guide by Nicholas J. Tate Read more at location 756
Did President Barack Obama "steal" $500 billion from Medicare?From <http://www.politifact.com/truth-o-meter/statements/2011/sep/12/michele-bachmann/did-president-obama-steal-500-billion-medicare/>
Nearly $220 billion comes from reducing annual increases in payments that health care providers would otherwise receive from Medicare. Other savings include $36 billion from increases in premiums for higher-income beneficiaries and $12 billion from administrative changes. A new national board -- the Independent Payment Advisory Board -- will be tasked to identify $15.5 billion in savings, but the board is prohibited from proposing anything that would ration care or reduce or modify benefits. Then there's another $136 billion in projected savings that would come from changes to the Medicare Advantage program, an alternative to traditional Medicare that has turned out to be much more costly than expected. About 25 percent of Medicare beneficiaries are enrolled in a Medicare Advantage plan.

220 ObamaCare Survival Guide by Nicholas J. Tate Read more at location 516

221 *Id.* at location 1169

222 AMAC E-mail dated 3/19/14

223 *Id.*

Health Care Reforms from the Affordable Care Act	Savings from law's enactment through 2016
Reducing excessive Medicare payments to private insurers who operate in Medicare Advantage	$68 billion
Reforming provider payments, including improved productivity	$85 billion
Improving patient safety through the Partnership for Patients	$10 billion through 2013*
Cracking down on fraud and abuse in the Medicare system, and getting the best value for Medicare beneficiaries and taxpayers for durable medical equipment	$7.8 billion**
Additional provisions, including the net effect of expanded benefits, lowered payments for hospital acquired conditions, readmissions reductions, and adjustment to premium subsidies	$41 billion

* Amount shown represents the reduction in Medicare expenditures that could be achieved if the CMS goals for reducing readmissions and hospital-acquired conditions are met

** Estimated savings for Medicare program integrity provisions in the Affordable Care Act, does not include other, ongoing CMS initiatives

http://www.cms.gov/apps/files/ACA-savings-report-2012.pdf

224 Then in July 2012, the CBO projected Medicare outlays would be reduced by about $716 billion between 2013 and 2022. Read more at location 515 ObamaCare Survival

Guide by Nicholas J. Tate

225 From <http://dailycaller.com/2013/01/14/raiding-medicare-how-seniors-will-pay-for-obamacare/>

226 Get the Facts on the Impact of ObamaCare on Medicare http://obamacarefacts.com/obamacare-medicare.php

227 Originally Posted At The Wall Street Journal By Lawrence A. Hunter and Peter Ferrara October 4, 2010 From <http://socialsecurityinstitute.com/blog/how-obamacare-guts-medicare>

228 Originally Posted At The Wall Street Journal By Lawrence A. Hunter and Peter Ferrara October 4, 2010 From <http://socialsecurityinstitute.com/blog/how-obamacare-guts-medicare>

229 ObamaCare Survival Guide by Nicholas J. Tate Read more at location 533

230 *Id.* at location 794

231 From <http://www.forbes.com/sites/theapothecary/2012/08/20/how-obamacares-716-billion-in-cuts-will-drive-doctors-out-of-medicare/>

232 From <http://www.forbes.com/sites/aroy/2012/10/02/the-ratio-of-obamacares-medicare-cuts-to-new-benefits-is-fifteen-to-one/>

Hence, Obamacare's increases in net spending on preventive care and the prescription-drug program amount to $52 billion from 2013-2022, according to the CBO. Offsetting this new spending is $768 billion in net Medicare cuts elsewhere, a ratio of 15 to 1.

233 From <http://www.forbes.com/sites/theapothecary/2012/08/16/fact-checking-the-obama-campaigns-defense-of-its-716-billion-cut-to-medicare/>

234 From <http://dailycaller.com/2013/01/14/raiding-medicare-how-seniors-will-pay-for-obamacare/2/>

235 The Decline and Fall of Medicare by Elaina F. George, MD From <http://www.nationalcenter.org/P21NVGeorgeMedicare91012.html>

236 *Id.*

237 Read the rest of this PolitiChicks.tv article here: http://politichicks.tv/column/latest-obamacare-glitch-dishonoring-americas-elderly/#ZQcqWWUvGWSdCX9V.99

238 Read the rest of this Liberty Alliance article here: http://libertyalliance.com/2014/04/latest-obamacare-glitch-dishonoring-americas-elderly/#yEMiTQCguEdrDb58.99

239 Cash for Obamacare Shirkers Michelle Malkin | May 14, 2014 From <http://townhall.com/columnists/michellemalkin/2014/05/14/cash-for-obamacare-shirkers-n1837752/page/full>

240 *Id.*

241 Study shows ObamaCare would cut Medicare services, providers posted at 9:00 am on November 15, 2009 by Ed Morrissey

242 *Id.*

243 Get the Facts on the Impact of ObamaCare on Medicare http://obamacarefacts.com/obamacare-medicare.php

244 *Id.*

245 The Truth About Obamacare (Sally C. Pipes)- Highlight Loc. 2019-20.

246 Republican Governors Hit Obama Administration on Medicare Advantage Rates Heather Ginsberg | Apr 18, 2014 http://townhall.com/tipsheet/heatherginsberg/2014/04/18/republican-governors-hit-obama-administration-on-medicare-advantage-rates-n1825760

247 *Id.*

248 *Id.*

249 *Id.*

250 ObamaCare Survival Guide by Nicholas J. Tate Read more at location 1923

251 Decoding the Obama Health Law: What you Need to know - Betsy McCaughey

Read more at location 651

[252] From <http://www.forbes.com/sites/theapothecary/2012/08/16/fact-checking-the-obama-campaigns-defense-of-its-716-billion-cut-to-medicare/>

[253] Delegated powers cannot be subdelegated. The U.S. Constitution vests all legislative powers in Congress, and all judicial powers in the Supreme Court and inferior courts, except as specifically expressed. Executive branch officials may subdelegate but must remain responsible for the actions of their subordinates. There can be no authority exercised that is not accountable through constitutional officials.*Delegata potestas non potest delegari.* A delegated power cannot be delegated. 9 Inst. 597. Constitutional Interpretation, https://www.thefederalistpapers.org/principles-of-constitutional-interpretation

[254] The Scheme behind the Obamacare Fraud, Andrew C. McCarthy, 11/23/13, National Review Online, http://www.nationalreview.com/article/364667/scheme-behind-obamacare-fraud-andrew-c-mccarthy

[255] From <https://www.nationalreview.com/nrd/articles/301164/acronym-ate-health-care>

[256] The Scheme behind the Obamacare Fraud Lies smooth the transition to a fundamental transformation of our health-care system. By Andrew C. McCarthy From <http://www.nationalreview.com/article/364667/scheme-behind-obamacare-fraud-andrew-c-mccarthy/page/0/1> November 23, 2013 4:00 AM

[257] Medicaid, the Next Obama Disaster Bruce Bialosky | Apr 27, 2014 http://townhall.com/columnists/brucebialosky/2014/04/27/medicaid-the-next-obama-disaster-n1828790?utm_source=thdaily&utm_medium=email&utm_campaign=nl

[258] The Truth About Obamacare (Sally C. Pipes)- Highlight Loc. 1202-3. And See Medicaid, the Next Obama Disaster Bruce Bialosky | Apr 27, 2014 http://townhall.com/columnists/brucebialosky/2014/04/27/medicaid-the-next-obama-disaster-n1828790?utm_source=thdaily&utm_medium=email&utm_campaign=nl

[259] Medicaid, the Next Obama Disaster Bruce Bialosky | Apr 27, 2014 http://townhall.com/columnists/brucebialosky/2014/04/27/medicaid-the-next-obama-disaster-n1828790?utm_source=thdaily&utm_medium=email&utm_campaign=nl

[260] Decoding the Obama Health Law: What you Need to know - Betsy McCaughey Read more at location 770

[261] *Id.* at location 432-33

[262] *Id.* at location 432

[263] *Id.* at location 437

[264] *Id.* at location 447

[265] *Id.* at location 451

[266] From <http://www.heritage.org/research/reports/2010/05/obamacare-impact-on-doctors>

[267] ObamaCare Survival Guide by Nicholas J. Tate Read more at location 1162

[268] From <http://www.heritage.org/research/reports/2010/05/obamacare-impact-on-doctors>

[269] Bobby Jindal: The liberal left's misplaced priorities on Medicaid expansion

[270] ObamaCare created a Medicaid time bomb By Michael D. Tanner December 7, 2013 | 9:15pm http://nypost.com/2013/12/07/the-medicaid-time-bomb/

[271] *Id.*

[272] *Id.*

[273] States to Seize Estates to Payback Cost of Medicaid by Dave Jolly From <http://godfatherpolitics.com/13727/states-seize-estates-payback-cost-medicaid/>

[274] H. R. 3590—pg. 444 Prevention or management of chronic disease

[275] *Id.*

[276] *Id.* at pg. 447

[277] ObamaCare Survival Guide by Nicholas J. Tate Read more at location 639

[278] Surprise (not): Health insurance premiums up to 56% higher under Obamacare Written by Allen West on March 19, 2014 From <http://allenbwest.com/2014/03/surprise-health-insurance-premiums-56-higher-obamacare/>

[279] Read more at http://www.westernjournalism.com/next-four-obamacare-disasters/#QyLxmTfDPRO4pluA.99

[280] *Id.*

[281] http://obamacarefacts.com/obamacare-smokers.php

[282] Decoding the Obama Health Law: What you Need to know - Betsy McCaughey Read more at location 814. "The Joint Committee and the CBO confirm that this tax will be passed on to consumers and raise their premiums, costing the average family $300 to $400 dollars a year in added premium costs."

[283] Insurance Company Lays Out Obamacare Tax Hikes Kevin Glass | Dec 27, 2013 From <http://townhall.com/tipsheet/kevinglass/2013/12/27/insurance-company-lays-out-obamacare-tax-hikes-n1768729?utm_source=thdailypm&utm_medium=email&utm_campaign=nl_pm>

[284] Bailing Out Health Insurers and Helping Obamacare 8:01 AM, Jan 13, 2014 • By JEFFREY H. ANDERSON From <http://www.weeklystandard.com/blogs/bailing-out-health-insurers-and-helping-obamacare_774167.html?page=2>

[285] *Id.*

[286] Obamacare Policies Not Available Year-Round, Causes Problems For Latecomers Posted on April 5, 2014 Read more at http://teapartyeconomist.com/2014/04/05/obamacare-policies-available-year-round-causes-problems-latecomers/#kIWTuEUH73TfXjRb.99

[287] Obamacare Architect: "Insurance Companies As We Know Them Are About to Die" Suzanne Hamner March 4, 2014 Read more at http://freedomoutpost.com/2014/03/obamacare-architect-insurance-companies-know-die/#SVPUHkk2iBOHFbQ8.99

[288] The Truth About Obamacare (Sally C. Pipes)- Highlight Loc. 1509-10

[289] From <http://www.foxnews.com/politics/2013/11/05/obamacare-price-hikes-hit-red-states-hardest/> ObamaCare price hikes hit 'red states' hardest By Maxim Lott Published November 05, 2013, quoting data from the Heritage Foundation.

[290] Estimate: 16 Million Americans Will Lose Current Coverage Because of Obamacare Guy Benson | Oct 24, 2013 From <http://townhall.com/tipsheet/guybenson/2013/14/24/estimate-16-million-americans-will-lose-current-coverage-because-of-obamacare-n1731700?utm_source=thdaily&utm_medium=email&utm_campaign=nl>

[291] From <http://washingtonexaminer.com/survey-finds-doctors-rebelling-against-obamacare-famous-hospitals-declining-to-join/article/2539830?utm_campaign=Fox%20News&utm_source=foxnews.com&utm_medium=feed>

[292] Nation's top cancer hospitals not covered under Obamacare By Howard Portnoy on March 20, 2014 at 11:42 am From <http://libertyunyielding.com/2014/03/20/nations-top-cancer-hospitals-covered-obamacare/>

[293] Congressional Research Service, 7-570 www.crs.gov R41159

[294] http://obamacarefacts.com/how-will-obamacare-affect-me.php

[295] About Obamacare (Sally C. Pipes)- Highlight Loc. 2338-41

[296] ObamaCare Survival Guide by Nicholas J. Tate Read more at location 704

[297] *Id.* at location 2493

[298] Report: Obamacare Will Leave Many Uninsured http://www.newsmax.com/InsiderReport/Solyndra-OilPipeline-Misguided-

Priorities/2011/12/04/id/419886/
[299] http://obamacarefacts.com/how-will-obamacare-affect-me.php
[300] HR 3950. SEC. 10108. FREE CHOICE VOUCHERS.
[301] 'A public safety disaster': Obamacare could force THOUSANDS of volunteer fire departments to close By David Martosko, U.s. Political Editor PUBLISHED: 15:58 EST, 9 December 2013 | UPDATED: 11:53 EST, 10 December 2013
[302] The Truth About Obamacare (Sally C. Pipes)- Highlight Loc. 1583-85
[303] *Id.*
[304] *Id.* at Loc. 1622-23
[305] ObamaCare Puts Big Dent in Hiring by John Rossomando 06/29/2011 Pasted from <http://www.humanevents.com/article.php?id=44535>
[306] CBO: Obamacare Driving Millions Out of Work Force, Price Tag Tops $2 Trillion Guy Benson | Feb 04, 2014 From <http://townhall.com/tipsheet/guybenson/2014/02/04/cbo-obamacare-driving-millions-of-americans-out-of-work-force-n1789435?utm_source=thdailypm&utm_medium=email&utm_campaign=nl_pm>
[307] Decoding the Obama Health Law: What you Need to know - Betsy McCaughey Read more at location 273
[308] *Id.* at location 278
[309] *Id.* at location 282
[310] From <http://godfatherpolitics.com/14334/companies-cant-fire-people-obamacare-costs/>
[311] From <http://townhall.com/tipsheet/katiepavlich/2013/10/31/health-insurance-losses-to-get-worse-with-employer-mandate-looming-n1733796?utm_source=thdailypm&utm_medium=email&utm_campaign=nl_pm>
[312] *Id.*
[313] Pasted from <http://www.gopusa.com/commentary/2012/03/16/limbaugh-obamas-health-care-duplicity-no-longer-debatable/?subscriber=1> Limbaugh: Obama's Health Care Duplicity No Longer Debatable By David Limbaugh March 16, 2012 6:55 am
[314] *Id.*
[315] From <http://www.nationalreview.com/article/364667/scheme-behind-obamacare-fraud-andrew-c-mccarthy/page/0/1> November 23, 2013 4:00 AM The Scheme behind the Obamacare Fraud
[316] Decision Points (George W. Bush)- Highlight Loc. 5512-13
[317] *Id.*
[318] The Truth About Obamacare (Sally C. Pipes) Page 213
[319] *Id.* at Loc. 1889-90
[320] Early Analysis: Obamacare Enrollees Take More HIV/AIDS, Pain Meds Than Privately Insured Sarah Jean Seman | Apr 09, 2014
[321] ObamaCare patients with serious pre-existing diseases could face expensive drug costs By Jim Angle Published February 15, 2014 From <http://www.foxnews.com/politics/2014/02/15/obamacare-patients-with-serious-pre-existing-diseases-could-face-expensive-drug/>
[322] The Truth About Obamacare (Sally C. Pipes)- Highlight Loc. 2107-9
[323] Decoding the Obama Health Law: What you Need to know - Betsy McCaughey Read more at location 581
[324] *Id.*
[325] HR 3930 pg 430
[326] The Truth About Obamacare (Sally C. Pipes)- Highlight Loc. 2603-4
[327] Decoding the Obama Health Law: What you Need to know - Betsy McCaughey Read more at location 673
[328] *Id.*

[329] ObamaCare Survival Guide by Nicholas J. Tate Read more at location 2345

[330] Report: 83 percent of doctors have considered quitting over Obamacare Published: 2:20 PM 07/09/2012 By Sally Nelson Pasted from <http://dailycaller.com/2012/07/09/report-83-percent-of-doctors-have-considered-quitting-over-obamacare/>

[331] H.R. 3950 -Pg 477 - (F) recommendations creating or revising national loan repayment programs and scholarship programs to require low-income, minority medical students to serve in their home communities, if designated as medical underserved community.

[332] From <http://www.heritage.org/research/reports/2010/05/obamacare-impact-on-doctors>

[333] Decoding the Obama Health Law: What you Need to know - Betsy McCaughey Read more at location 908

[334] *Id.* at location 897

[335] OBAMACARE DECLARES WAR ON DOCTORS From <http://dickmorris.rallycongress.com/5420/obamacare-declares-war-on-doctors/>

[336] *Id.*

[337] http://www.jdjournal.com/2014/04/09/medicare-physician-payments-data-released/?utm_source=MCNA&utm_medium=Email&utm_campaign=t_17740--dt_20140411-cid_34270-Did_5100191-ad_JDJ~MCNA#

[338] From <http://www.nationalcenter.org/NPA640.html>

[339] Read more at http://www.westernjournalism.com/next-four-obamacare-disasters/#QvLxmTfDPRO4pIuA.99

[340] http://townhall.com/tipsheet/katiepavlich/2014/03/24/how-much-youve-paid-to-promote-obamacare-n1813699

[341] Manipulating Obamacare Stats: The Census Bureau's Suspect Timing Guy Benson | Apr 15, 2014 http://townhall.com/tipsheet/guybenson/2014/04/15/cooking-the-books-the-census-bureaus-suspect-timing-n1824853

[342] *Id.*

[343] *Id.*

[344] http://www.jdjournal.com/2014/04/09/medicare-physician-payments-data-released/?utm_source=MCNA&utm_medium=Email&utm_campaign=t_17740--dt_20140411-cid_34270-Did_5100191-ad_JDJ~MCNA#

[345] Obamacare Propaganda in TV Scripts? Brent Bozell | Apr 04, 2014 From <http://townhall.com/columnists/brentbozell/2014/04/04/obamacare-propaganda-in-tv-scripts-n1818639/page/2>

[346] http://www.theblaze.com/stories/2014/03/30/snls-obama-does-something-with-justin-bieber-that-might-be-impossible-to-erase-from-memory/

[347] *Id.*

[348]http://www.realclearpolitics.com/articles/2013/11/22/remembering_stanley_ann_dunham_obama_120748.html

[349] *Id.*

[350] Healthcare.gov Can't Verify Barack Obama's Identity Posted By Tim Brown on Dec 24, 2013 From <http://freedomoutpost.com/2013/12/healthcare-gov-cant-identify-barack-obama-staff-attempts-sign-obamacare/>

[351] Group Receives $1.1 Million Grant to Gather Obamacare Success Stories Leah Barkoukis | Nov 29, 2013 From <http://townhall.com/tipsheet/leahbarkoukis/2013/11/29/group-gets-11-million-grant-to-collect-obamacare-success-stories-n1754649?utm_source=thdailypm&utm_medium=email&utm_campaign=nl_pm>

[352] Feds push students to promote Obamacare to their families Tuesday, August 06, 2013 by: Ethan A. Huff, staff writer

[353] *Id.*

[354] Struggling LAUSD students to be taught about Obamacare rather than how to read, write http://www.naturalnews.com/041506_obamacare_institutionalization_public_schools.html#ixzz2uRacp9Gn

[355] Struggling LAUSD students to be taught about Obamacare rather than how to read, write http://www.naturalnews.com/041506_obamacare_institutionalization_public_schools.html#ixzz2uRacp9Gn

[356] Report: Obama Admin Funded Obamacare Internet Propaganda Campaign Posted on August 19, 2011 at 4:14pm by Buck Sexton Pasted from <http://www.theblaze.com/stories/report-white-house-funded-obamacare-internet-propaganda-campaign/> and see http://www.judicialwatch.org/press-room/press-releases/judicial-watch-uncovers-new-documents-obama-administration-bankrolls-massive-internet-propaganda-campaign-to-push-obamacare/

[357] Report: Obama Admin Funded Obamacare Internet Propaganda Campaign Posted on August 19, 2011 at 4:14pm by Buck Sexton Pasted from <http://www.theblaze.com/stories/report-white-house-funded-obamacare-internet-propaganda-campaign/>

[358] Michelle Obama: Young People are Clearly "Knuckleheads" – That's Why They Need Obamacare Tim Brown Read more at http://freedomoutpost.com/2014/02/michelle-obama-young-people-clearly-knuckleheads-need-obamacare/#2sQezd1PbIGS6P19.99

[359] http://www.foxnews.com/politics/2014/02/04/new-obamacare-ads-to-reportedly-use-pets-to-target-young-women/

[360] How Do You Kill 11 Million People?: Why the Truth Matters More Than You Think by Andy Andrews location 382

[361] How Do You Kill 11 Million People?: Why the Truth Matters More Than You Think by Andy Andrews location 222

[362] *Id.* at location 229

[363] Executive Orders & Internment Camps: The Groundwork Has Been Laid for Martial Law in the Event of a National Emergency, by Richard Anthony March 6, 2014, From <http://freedomoutpost.com/2014/03/executive-orders-internment-camps-groundwork-laid-martial-law-event-national-emergency/>

[364] *Id.*

[365] Obamacare Labor Camps Under Construction In Multiple American States From <http://nationalreport.net/obamacare-labor-camps-construction-multiple-american-states/>

[366] *Id.*

[367] http://rt.com/usa/dhs-ammo-investigation-napolitano-645/

[368] *Id.*

[369] How Do You Kill 11 Million People?: Why the Truth Matters More Than You Think by Andy Andrews location 271

[370] FDA approves computer chip for humans. Devices could help doctors with stored medical information Associated Press, updated 10/13/2004 6:38:52 PM ET http://www.nbcnews.com/id/6237364/#.U0bqbldNv5E

[371] http://freedomoutpost.com/2013/01/obamas-executive-action-23-new-directives-with-the-stroke-of-a-pen/

[372] Proposed ATF Regulations, by Michael Connelly, Michael Connelly blog

[373] Federal Trade Commission v. American Tobacco Co. 262 U.S. 276 (1923)

[374] http://www.law.cornell.edu/wex/privacy

[375] 5 U.S.C. § 552a

[376] Obama administration releases updated online privacy policy Published April 18,

2014 FoxNews.com http://www.foxnews.com/politics/2014/04/18/obama-administration-releases-updated-online-privacy-policy/
[377] *Id.*
[378] H. R. 3590—462
''(b) DATA ANALYSIS.— ''(1) IN GENERAL.—For each federally conducted or supported health care or public health program or activity, the Secretary shall analyze data collected under paragraph (a) to detect and monitor trends in health disparities (as defined for purposes of section 485E) at the Federal and State levels.
''(c) DATA REPORTING AND DISSEMINATION.—
''(1) IN GENERAL.—The Secretary shall make the analyses described in (b) available to—
''(A) the Office of Minority Health;
''(B) the National Center on Minority Health and Health Disparities;
''(C) the Agency for Healthcare Research and Quality;
''(D) the Centers for Disease Control and Prevention;
''(E) the Centers for Medicare & Medicaid Services;
''(F) the Indian Health Service and epidemiology centers funded under the Indian Health Care Improvement Act;
''(G) the Office of Rural health;
''(H) other agencies within the Department of Health and Human Services; and
''(I) other entities as determined appropriate by the Secretary.
''(2) REPORTING OF DATA.—The Secretary shall report data and analyses described in (a) and (b) through—
''(A) public postings on the Internet websites of the Department of Health and Human Services; and
''(B) any other reporting or dissemination mechanisms determined appropriate by the Secretary.
''(3) AVAILABILITY OF DATA.—The Secretary may make data described in (a) and (b) available for additional research, analyses, and dissemination to other Federal agencies, non-governmental entities, and the public, in accordance with any Federal agency's data user agreements.
[379] *Id.* at (B)(3)
[380] http://conservativeamericaonline.blogspot.com/2014/02/video-convicted-terrorist-worked-as.html?utm_source=America%27s+Conservative+News&utm_campaign=283020900a-RSS_EMAIL_CAMPAIGN&utm_medium=email&utm_term=0_c28c63c891-283020900a-257128958#more ;
Read more at http://godfatherpolitics.com/13170/obamacare-providing-personal-info-convicted-felons/#IRm7GvS8yC2YIFTh.99
On Wednesday, Kathleen Sebelius, Secretary of Health and Human Services, was testifying before the Senate Finance Committee. They were grilling her on all of the problems associated with Obamacare. During the hearing, there was a short discourse between Sen. John Cornyn (R-TX) and Sebelius and it went like this:

> Cornyn: "Isn't it true that there is no federal requirement for navigators to undergo a criminal background check."
> Sebelius: "That is true. States could add in additional background checks and other features, but it is not part of the federal requirement."
> Cornyn: "So a convicted felon could be a navigator and could acquire sensitive personal information from an individual unbeknownst to them?"
> Sebelius: "This is possible."

[381] http://www.factcheck.org/2013/12/eric-cantors-security-scare/
[382] http://dailycaller.com/2013/10/03/john-mcafee-on-obamacare-this-is-a-hackers-wet-

dream-video/

[383] VA Data Breach Compromises Veteran's Private Information While Using Facebook John DeMayo Read more at http://freedomoutpost.com/2014/02/va-data-breach-compromises-veterans-private-information-using-facebook/#piEGV27SOEPpRRMm.99

[384] HR 3590 pg 778

[385] HR 3590, 1303(4)

[386] Sebelius v. Hobby Lobby Stores, Inc., and Conestoga Wood Specialties Corp. v. Sebelius Nos. 13-354 & 13-356.

[387] Citizens United v. Federal Election Commission 130 S. Ct. 876.

[388] Dick Morris: Democrats Conspiring to Rig Electoral College, Law Passed in 9 States So Far Tuesday, 15 Apr 2014 09:26 AM By Dick Morris http://www.newsmax.com/Morris/morris-democrats-electoral-college/2014/04/15/id/565661#ixzz2yz50SEoz

[389] Great by Choice: Uncertainty, Chaos, and Luck--Why Some Thrive Despite Them All. By Jim Collins, Read more at location 168

[390] *Id.* at location 328

[391] *Id.* at location 361-63

[392] *Id.* Great by Choice: Uncertainty, Chaos, and Luck--Why Some Thrive Despite Them All. By Jim Collins,

[393] *Id.*

[394] *Id.* at location 579-81

[395] *Id.* at location 1732

[396] *Id.* at location 2493

[397] *Id.* at location 3217

[398] *Id.* at location 2515

[399] *Id.* at location 1792

[400] Decision Points (George W. Bush)- Highlight Loc. 5476-77

[401] The Truth About Obamacare (Sally C. Pipes)- Highlight Loc. 1627-29

[402] *Id.* at Loc. 1889-90

[403] *Id.* at Loc. pp 211-217

[404] Obamacare Architect: "Insurance Companies As We Know Them Are About to Die" Suzanne Hamner March 4, 2014 Read more at http://freedomoutpost.com/2014/03/obamacare-architect-insurance-companies-know-die/#SVPUHkk2iBOHFbQ8.99

[405] http://usgovinfo.about.com/od/thepoliticalsystem/a/electcollege_2.htm

www.ingramcontent.com/pod-product-compliance
Lightning Source LLC
Chambersburg PA
CBHW060023210326
41520CB00009B/978

* 9 7 8 0 6 9 2 2 2 7 0 9 1 *